Chapter 1
The Mysterious Book Of Magic

Illustration:-
"The Mysterious Book Of Magic" opens with a scene that is both cozy and welcoming.

This book tells a sweet tale of a new mother who becomes upset with her fussy infant and tries to discover a way to soothe her down.

This book presents a charming fairytale picture of the existence of good magic but there are no signs of evil magic.

Overall, the book features some really lovely images that shows how a mother learns about the magic book, when she does, and what happens next. While the stardust and moonlight fantasy creates the illusion of being in a fairytale world, it actually conveys the message that you should establish a bedtime ritual for your child in order to prepare them for a restful and wonderful night.

Once upon a time, in a cozy little town nestled between rolling hills and whispering forests,

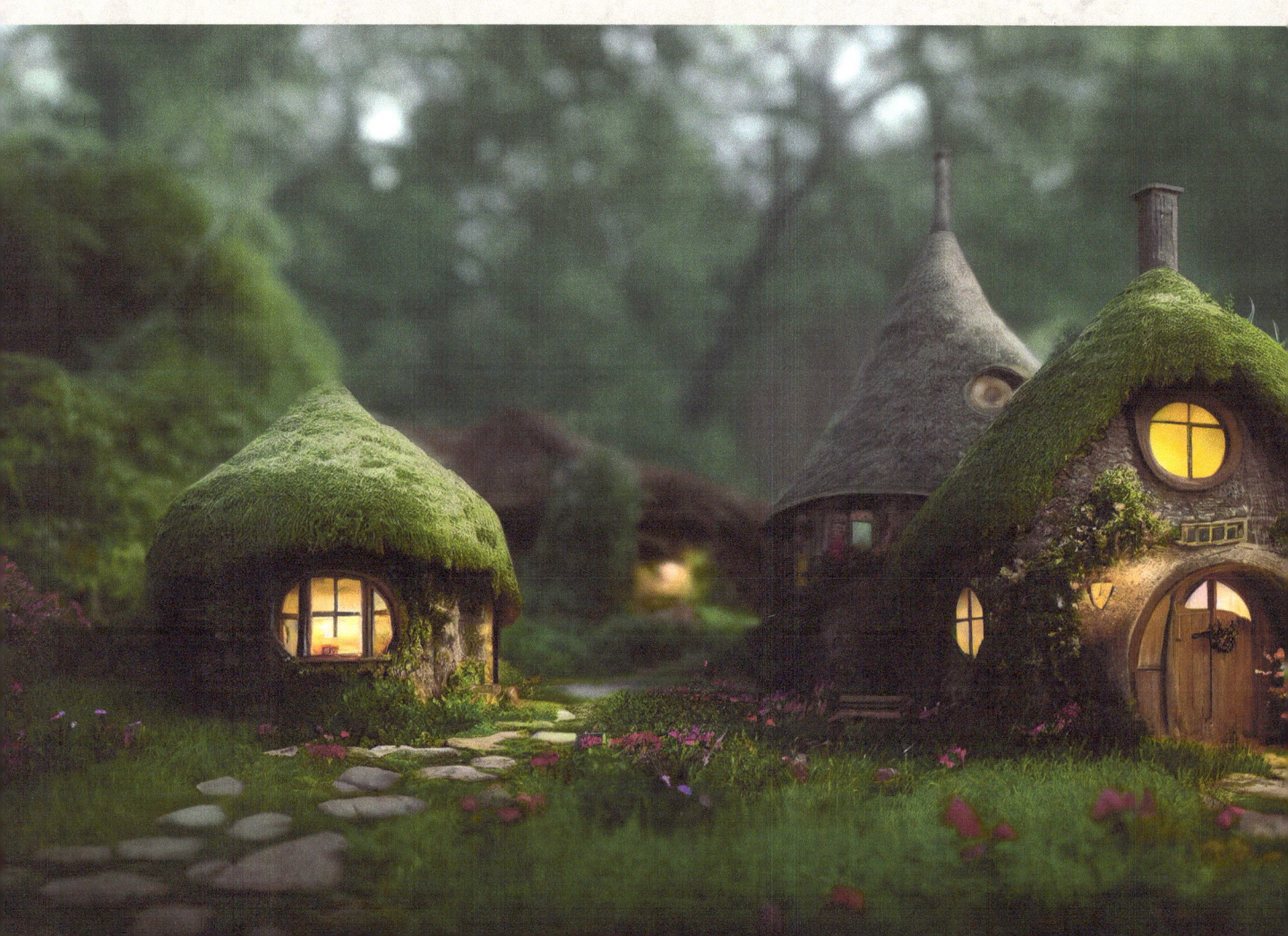

there was a quaint old bookstore named "Elderwood Mysteries."

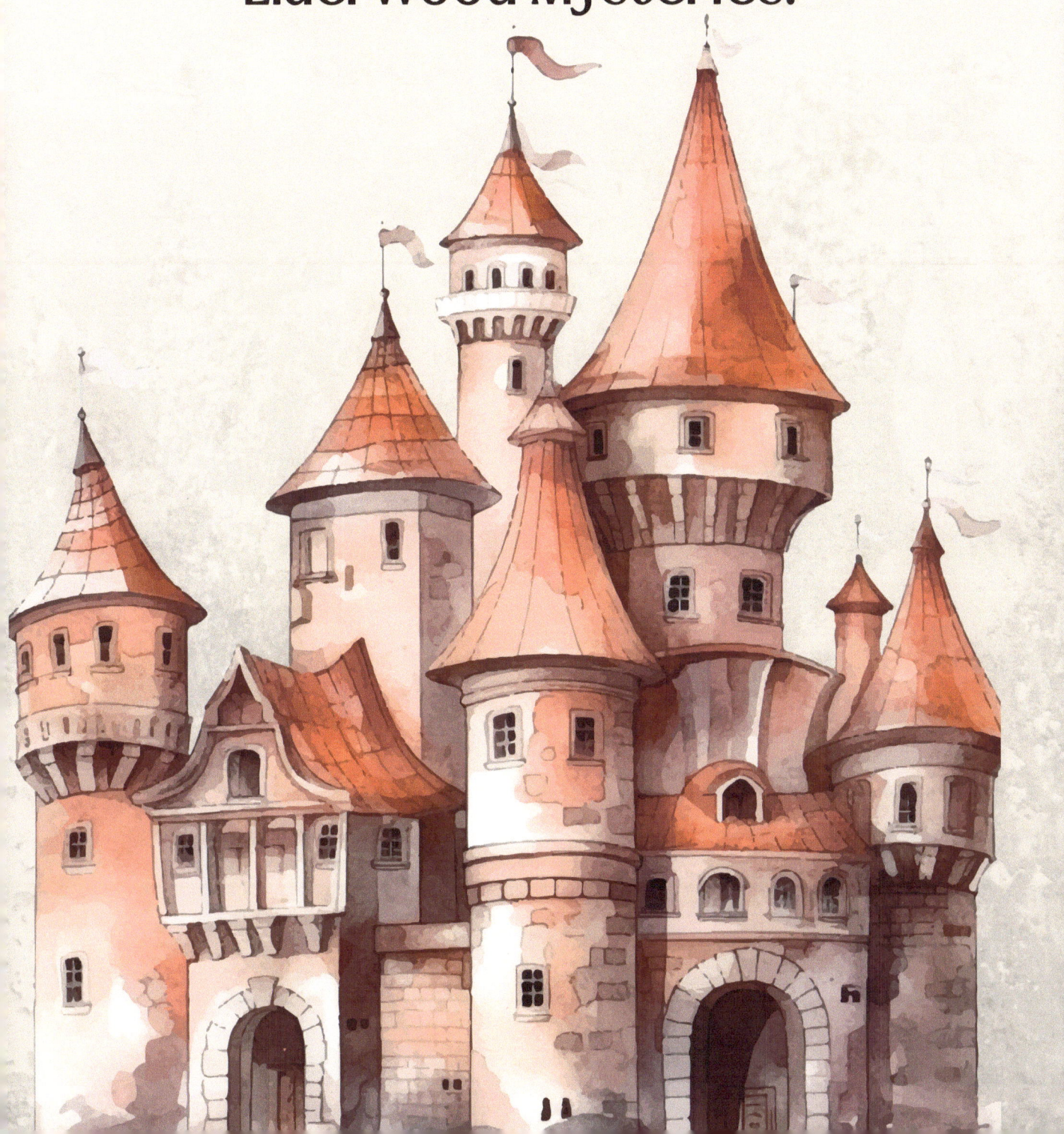

It was said that the books within its ancient shelves held secrets and wonders beyond imagining.

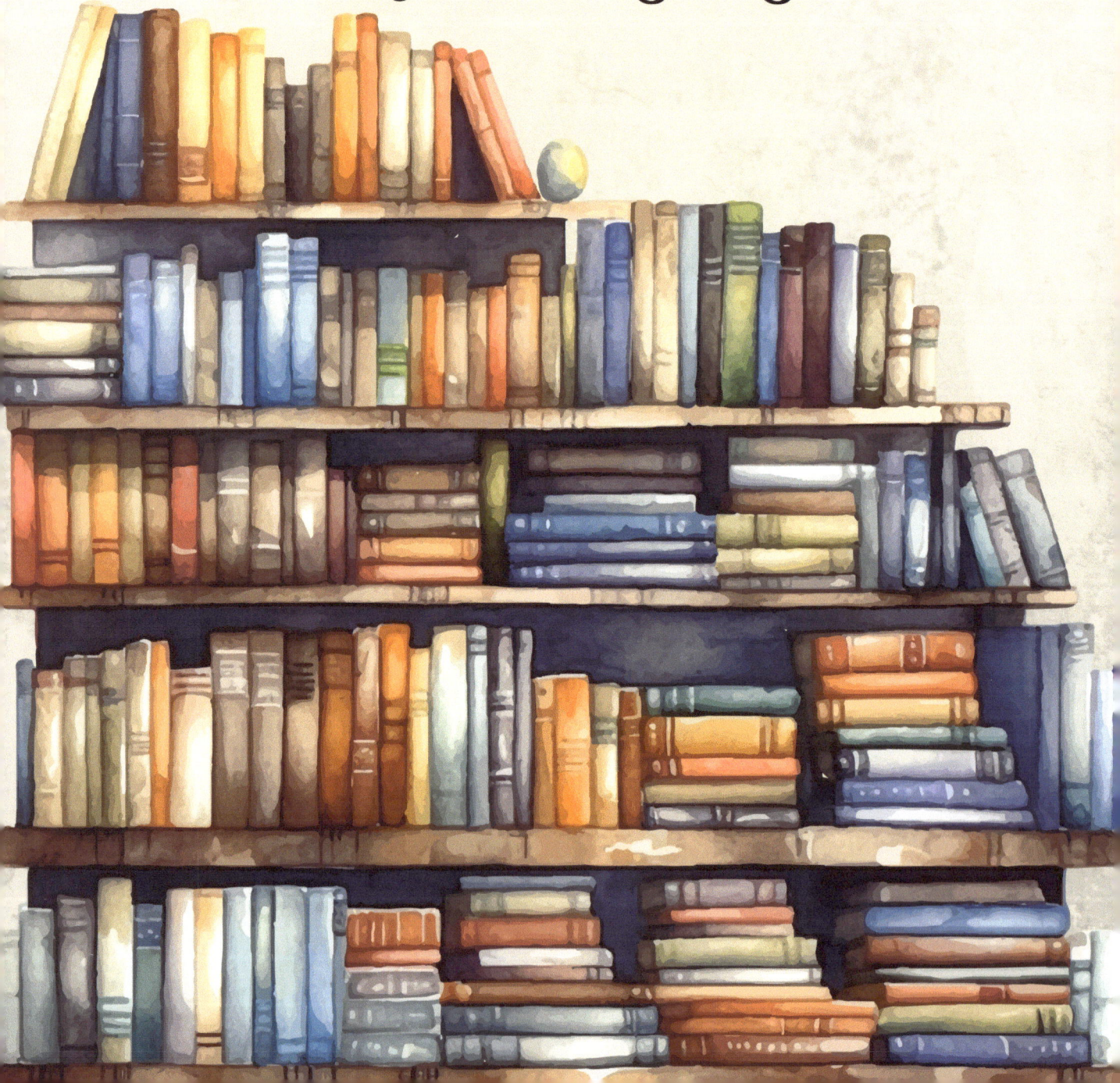

But there was one book that stood out among them all—a mysterious tome known simply as "The Book of Baby Magic."

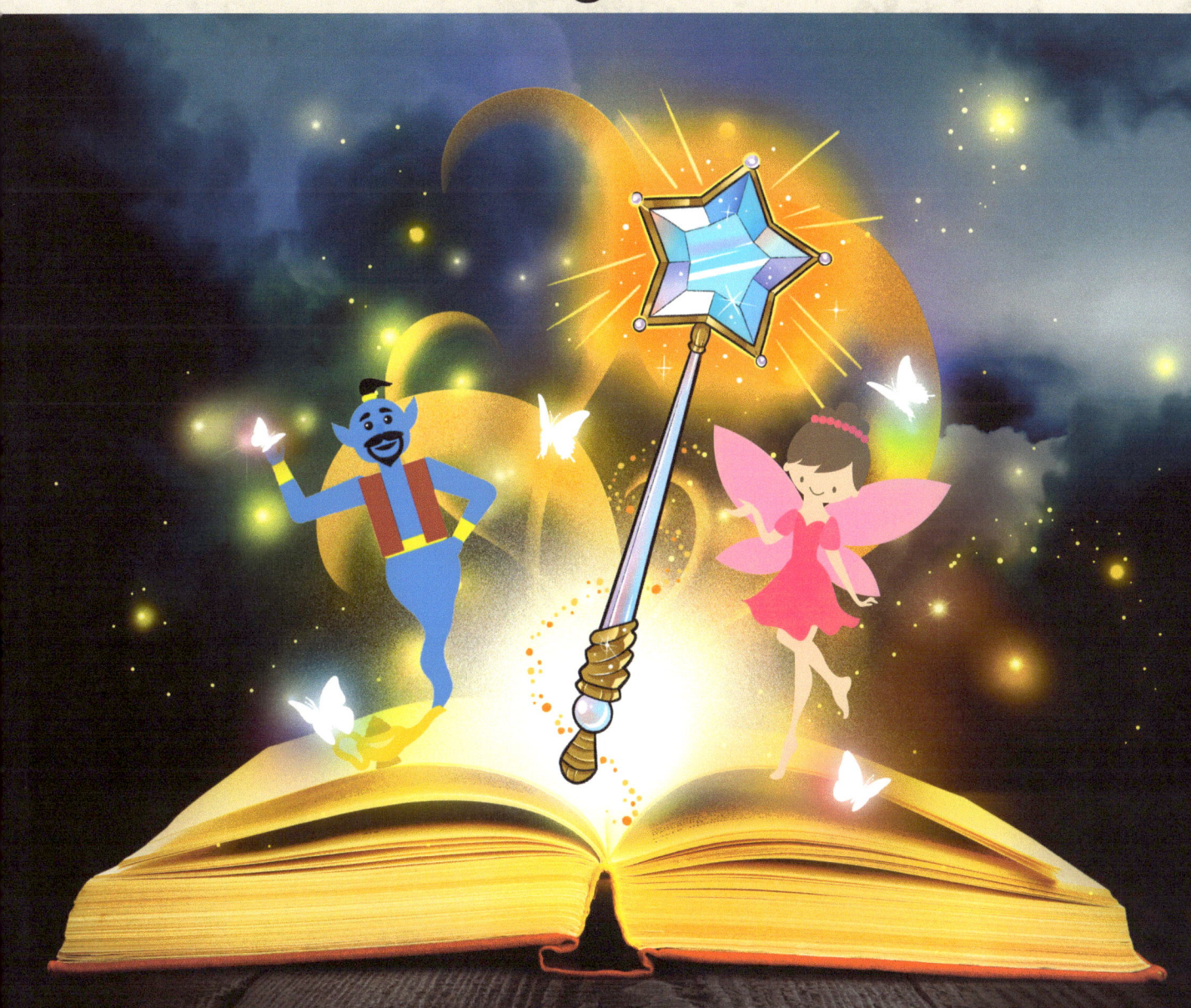

According to legend, this book was charmed to astonish even the smallest readers by being fashioned from moonbeams and stardust by the softest forest nymphs.

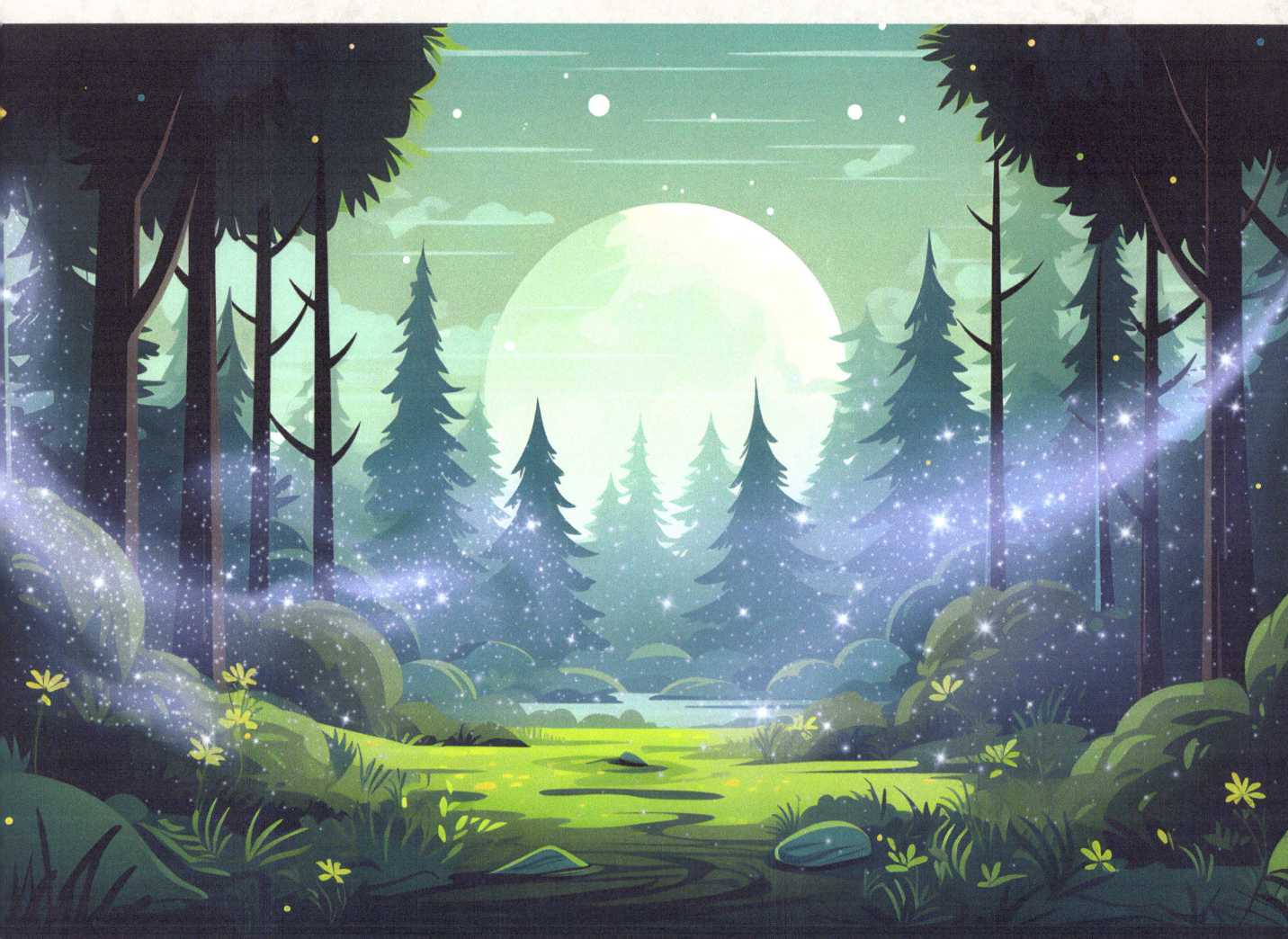

It was said that within its pages lay spells so gentle, so pure, that they could bring smiles to the faces of even the fussiest of babes.

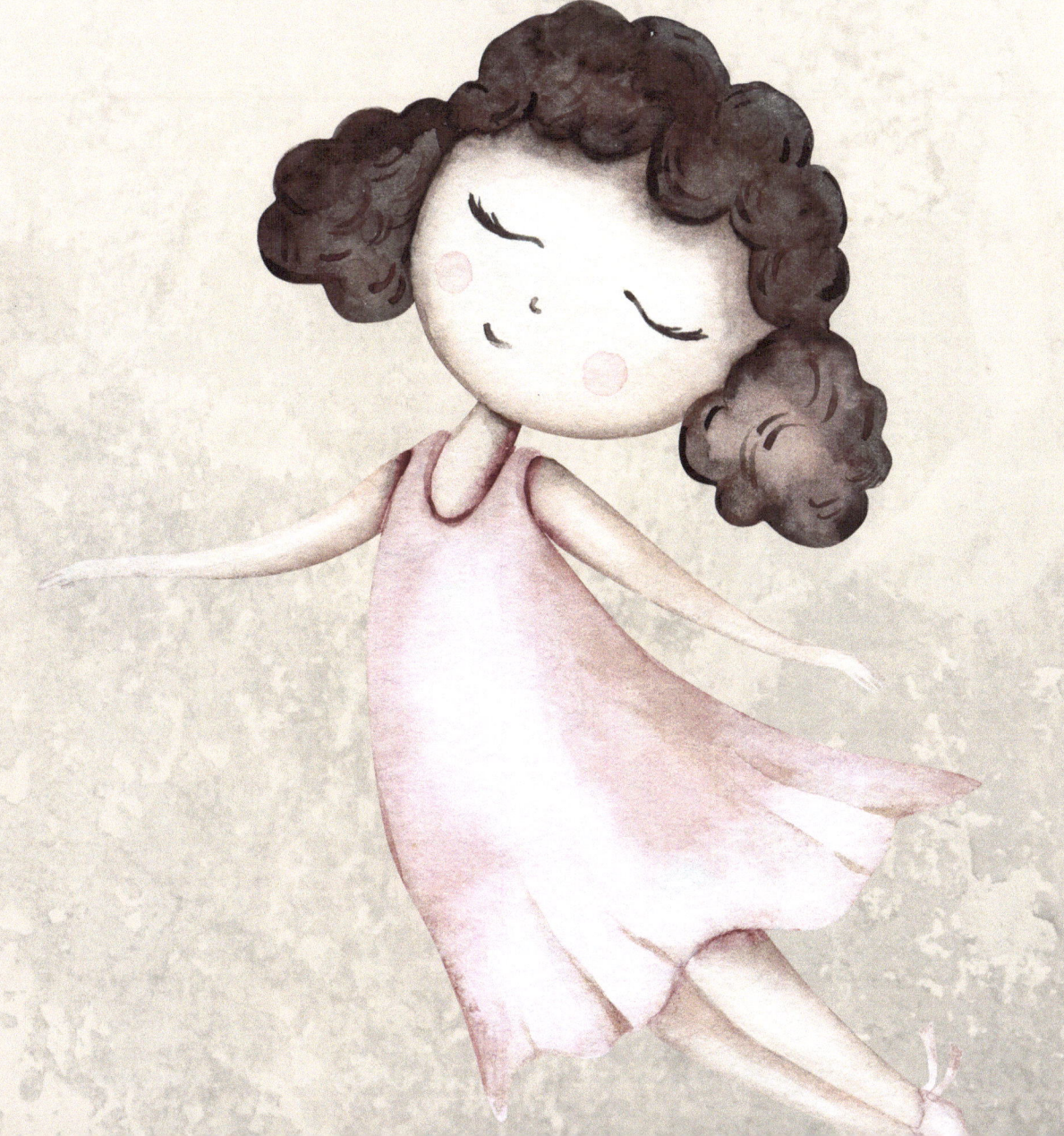

One evening, as the stars twinkled overhead and the crickets sang their lullabies, a young mother named Lily stumbled upon Elderwood Mysteries.

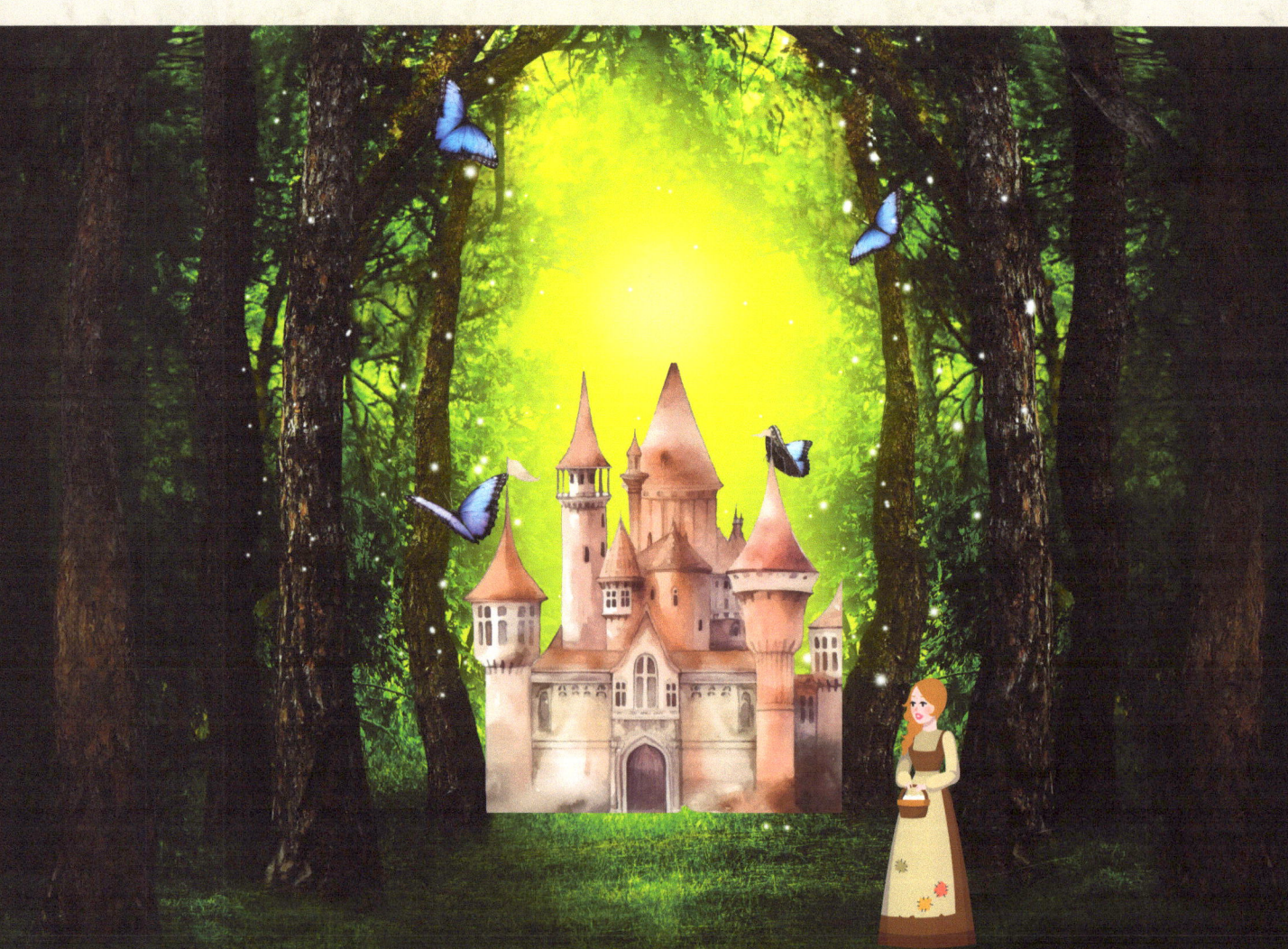

She was seeking
something special to
soothe her restless little
one, Emily, whose cries
echoed through their
cottage every night.

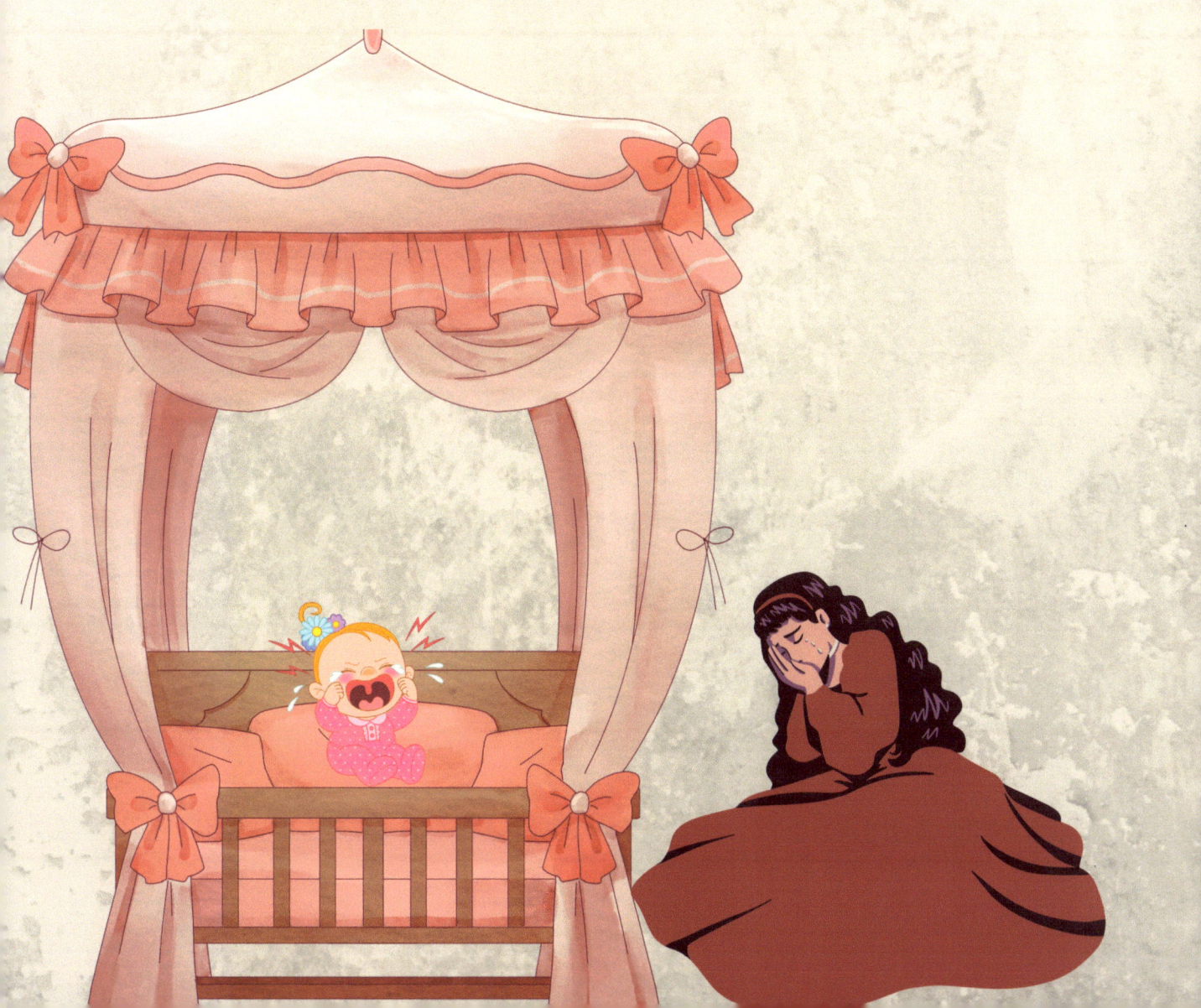

With a hopeful heart, Lily stepped inside the dimly lit shop, where the scent of old parchment and dried herbs filled the air.

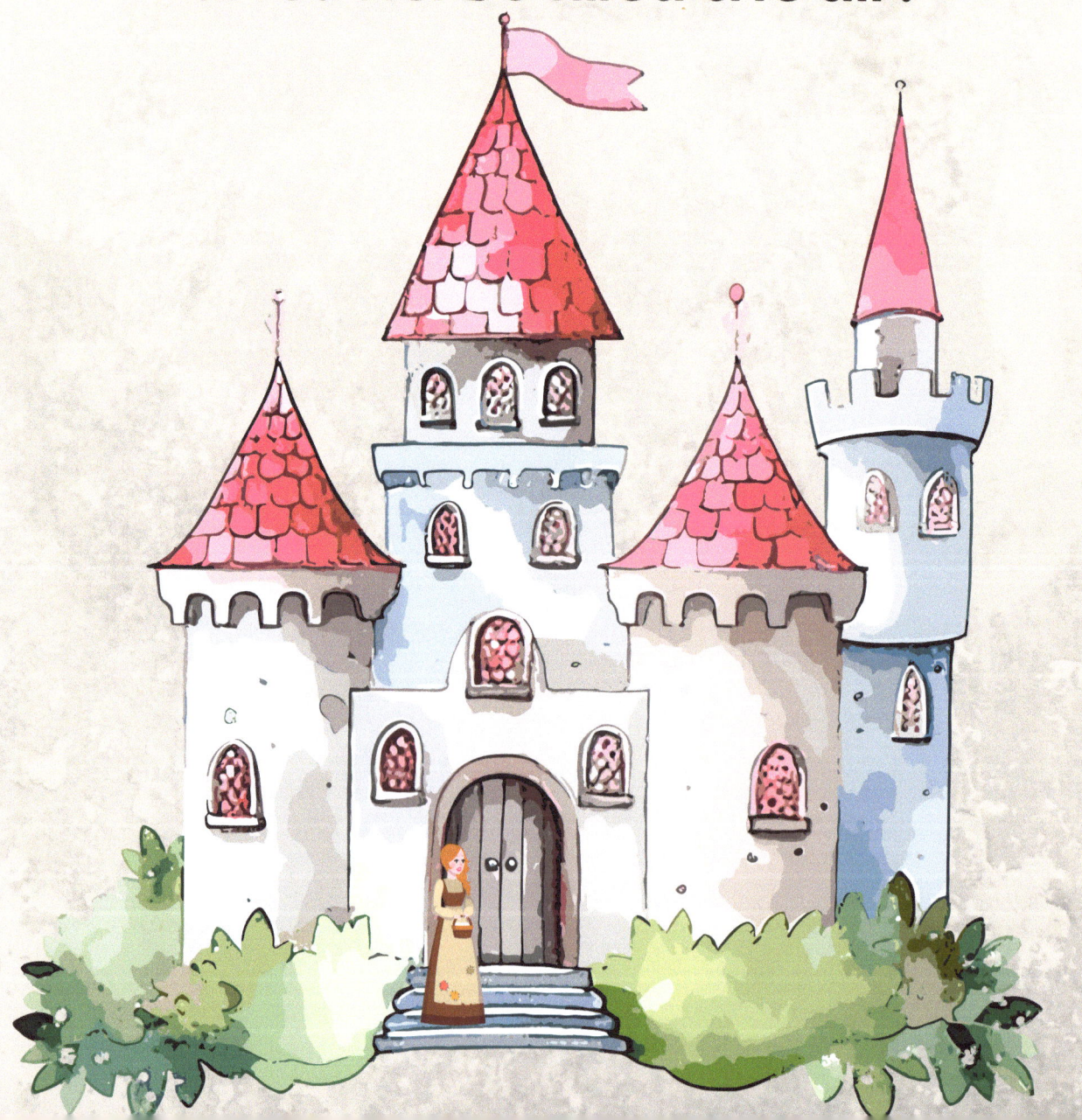

She was greeted by the kind bookseller, Mr. Hawthorne, who sensed her weary soul and offered her a warm smile.

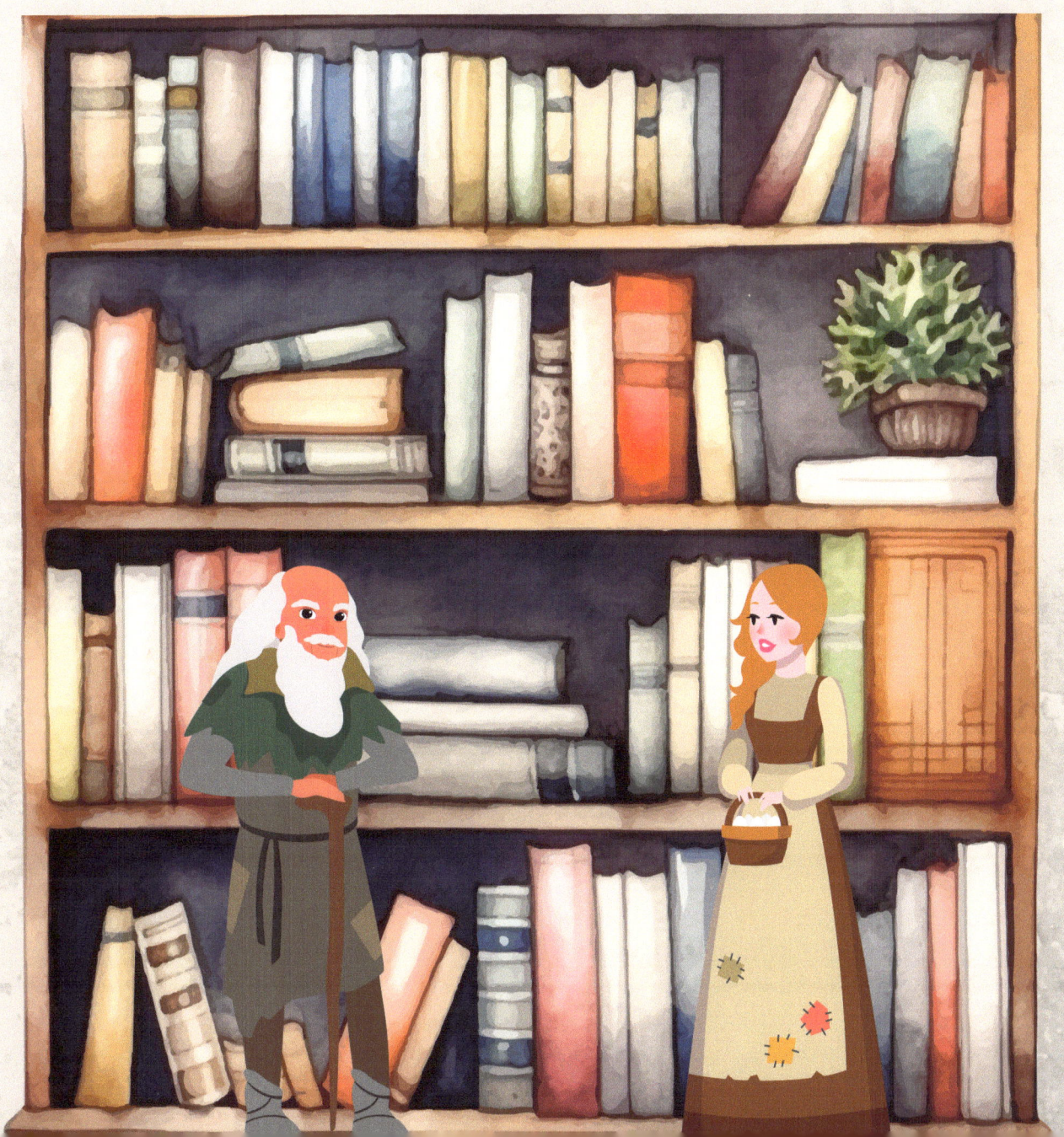

"I seek something magical," Lily whispered, her voice barely above a breath. "Something to quiet my baby's tears and fill her dreams with wonder."

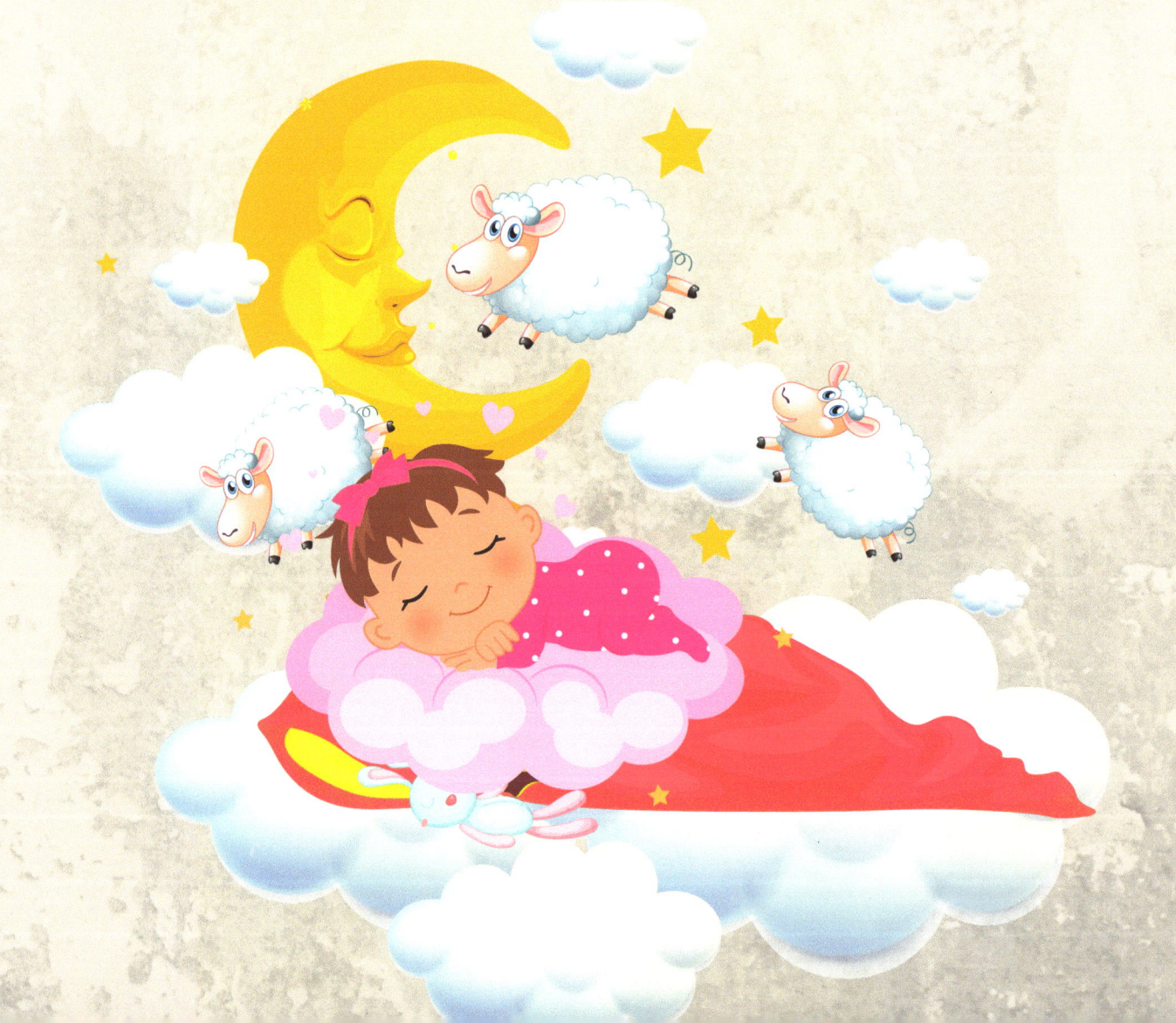

Mr. Hawthorne's eyes twinkled knowingly as he led her to a dusty corner of the shop,

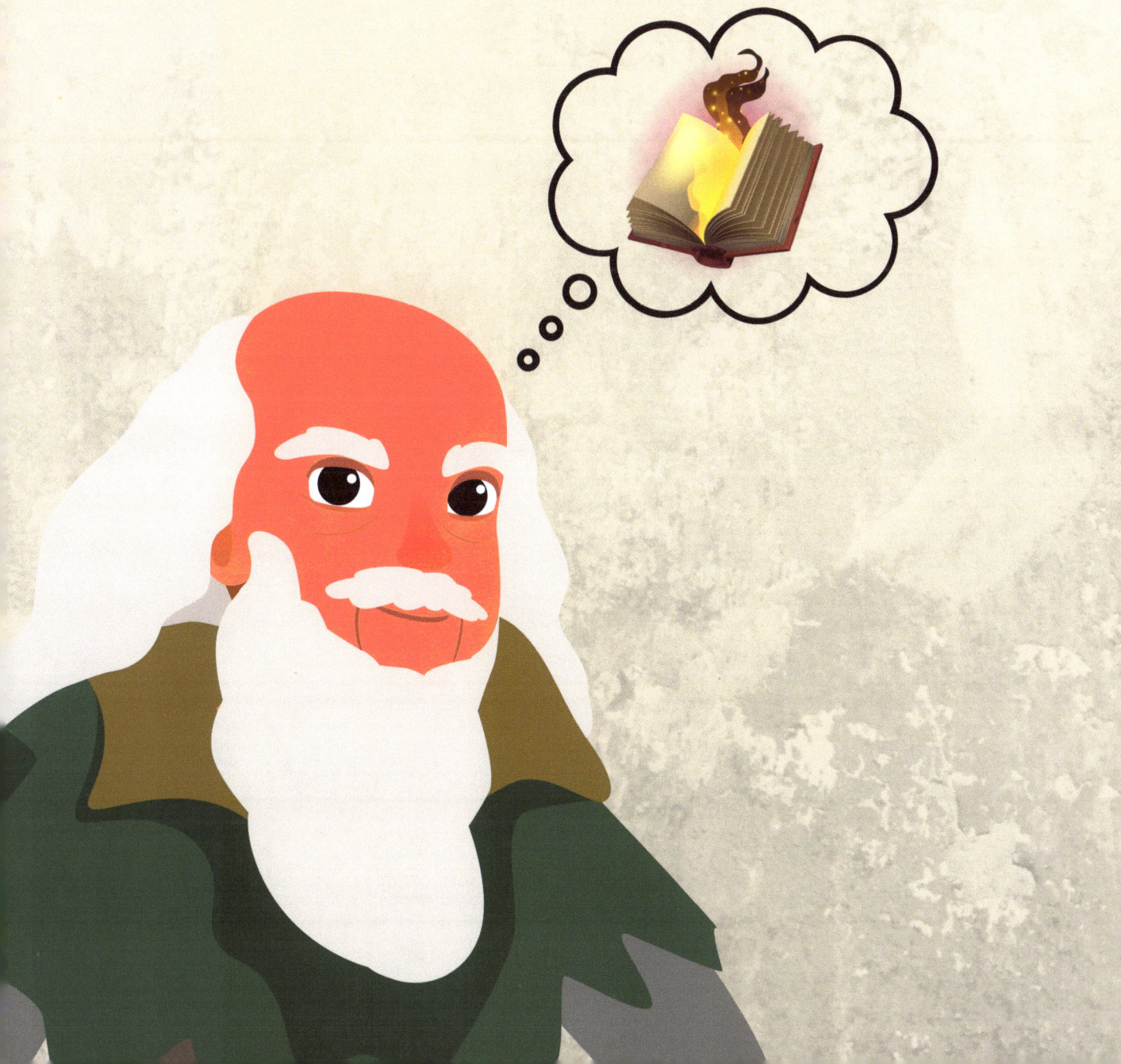

where the Book of Baby Magic
lay nestled among forgotten
tomes and cobwebs.

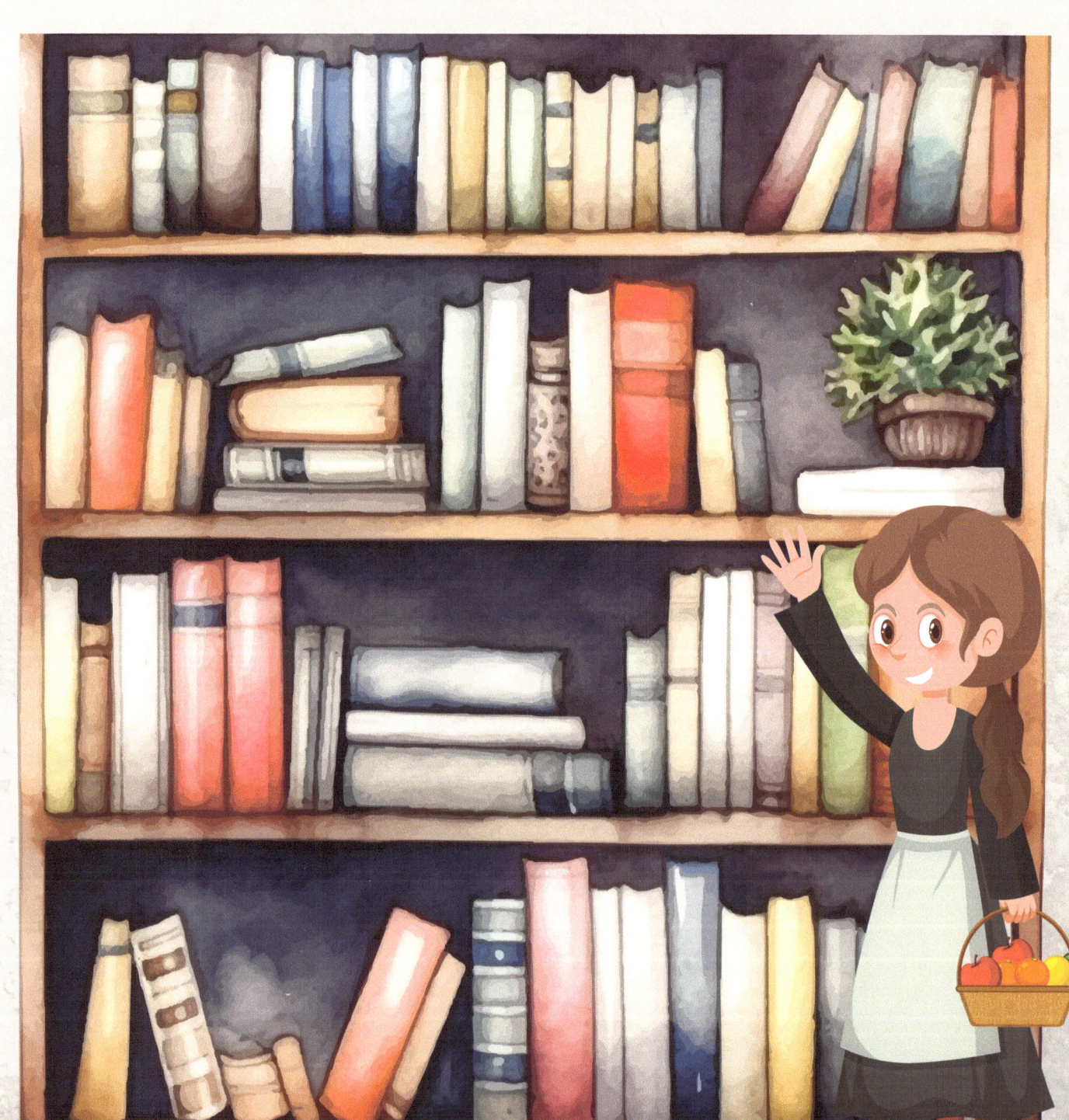

With trembling hands, Lily opened its weathered cover, and as she read its pages by the flickering light of the lantern, she felt a sense of enchantment wash over her.

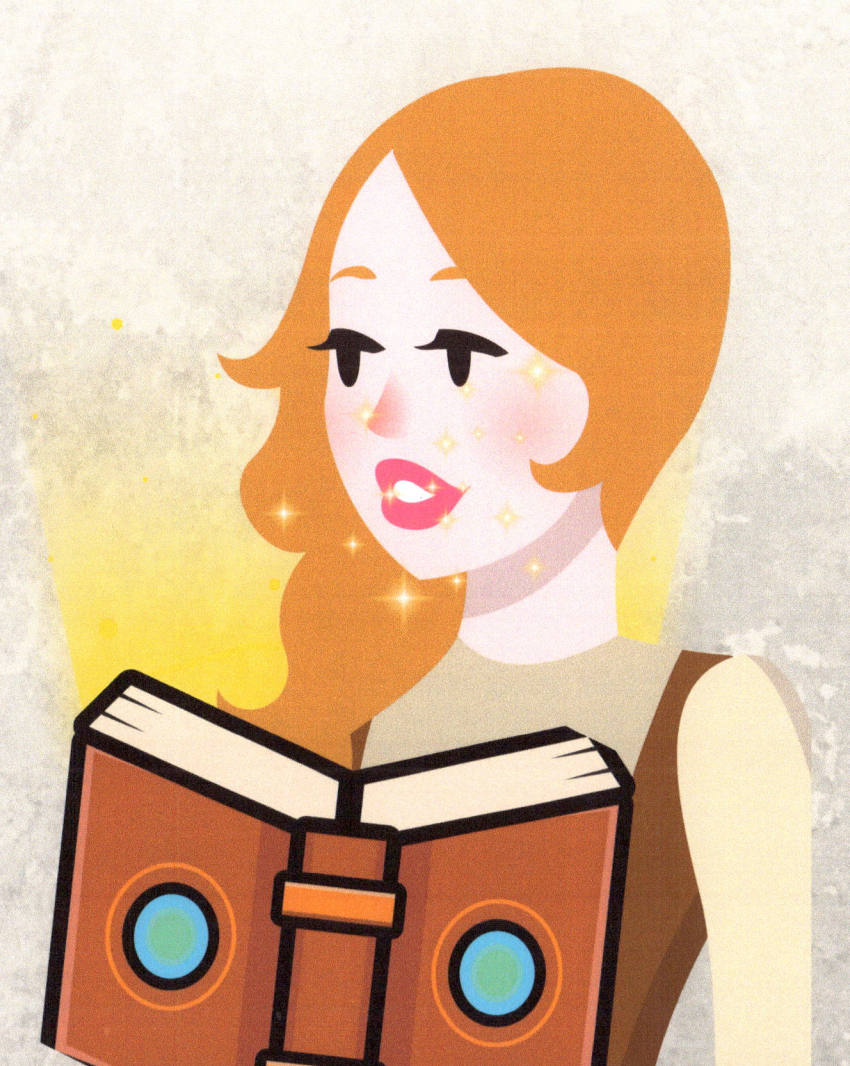

The book was filled with gentle rhymes and whimsical illustrations, each page adorned with soft, pastel hues that seemed to dance in the dim light.

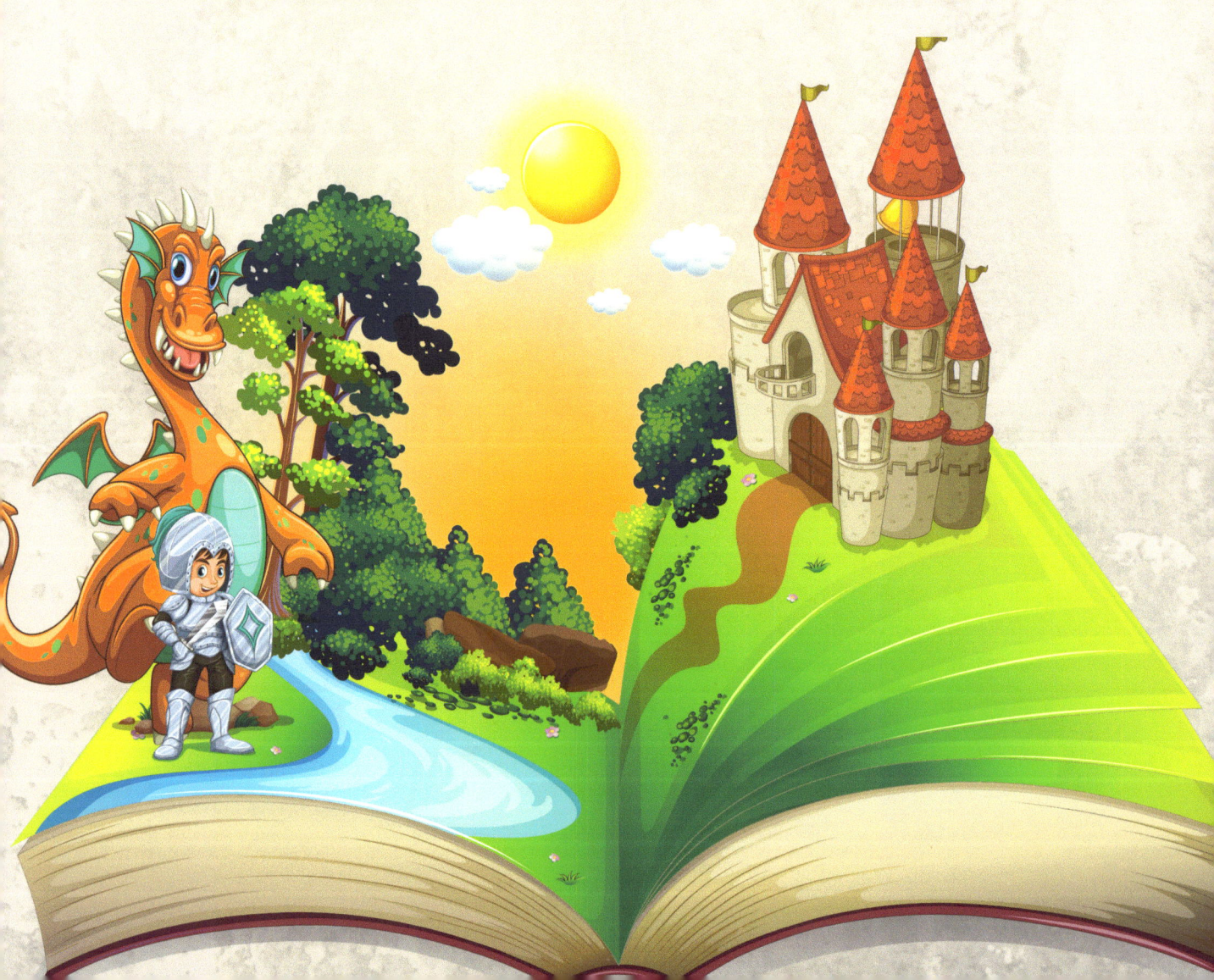

There were spells for soothing restless nights, charms for chasing away shadows, and lullabies that whispered secrets of the stars.

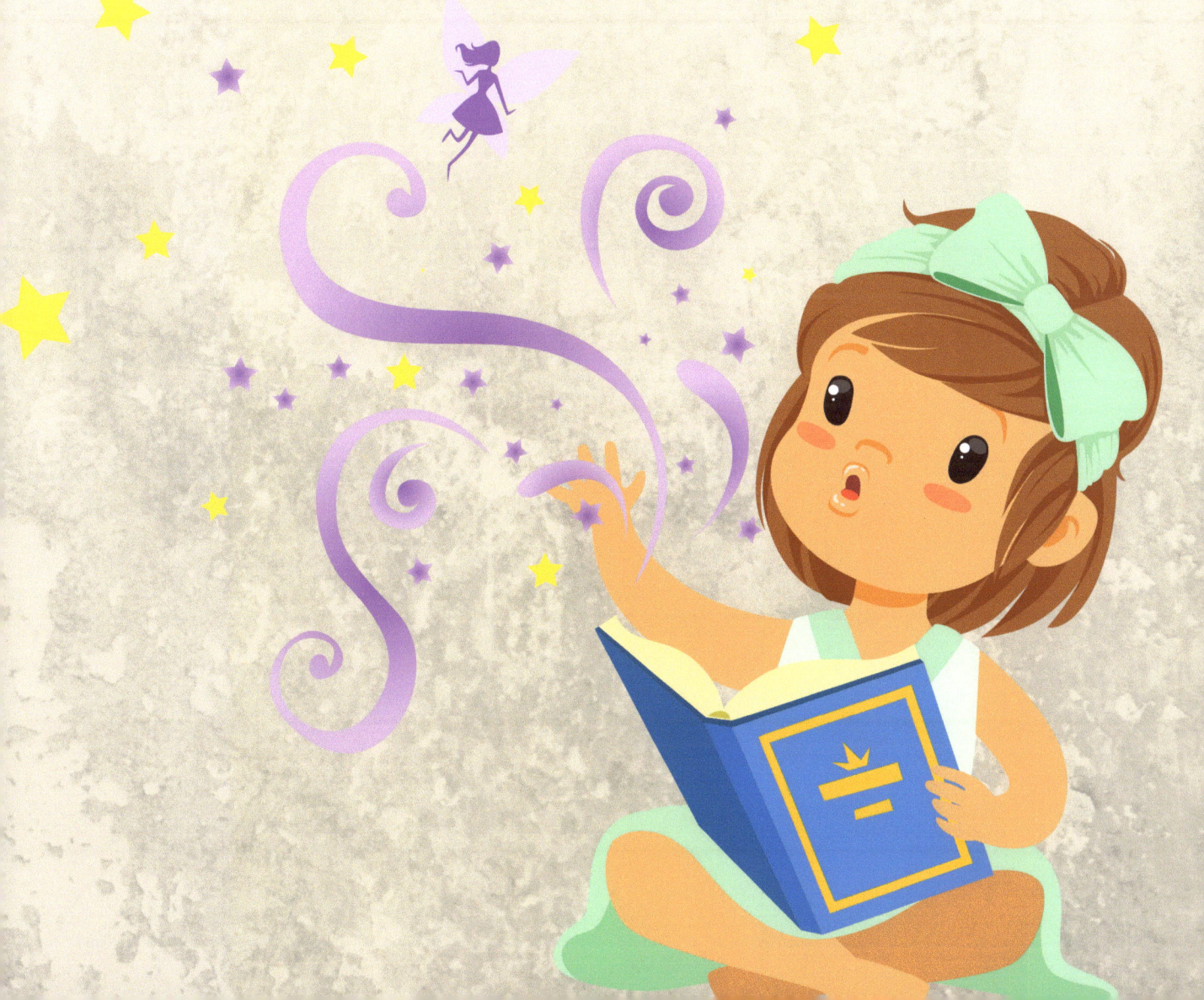

With a grateful smile, Lily tucked the book under her arm and hurried home to Emily's cradle, where the babe lay tossing and turning in the moonlit room.

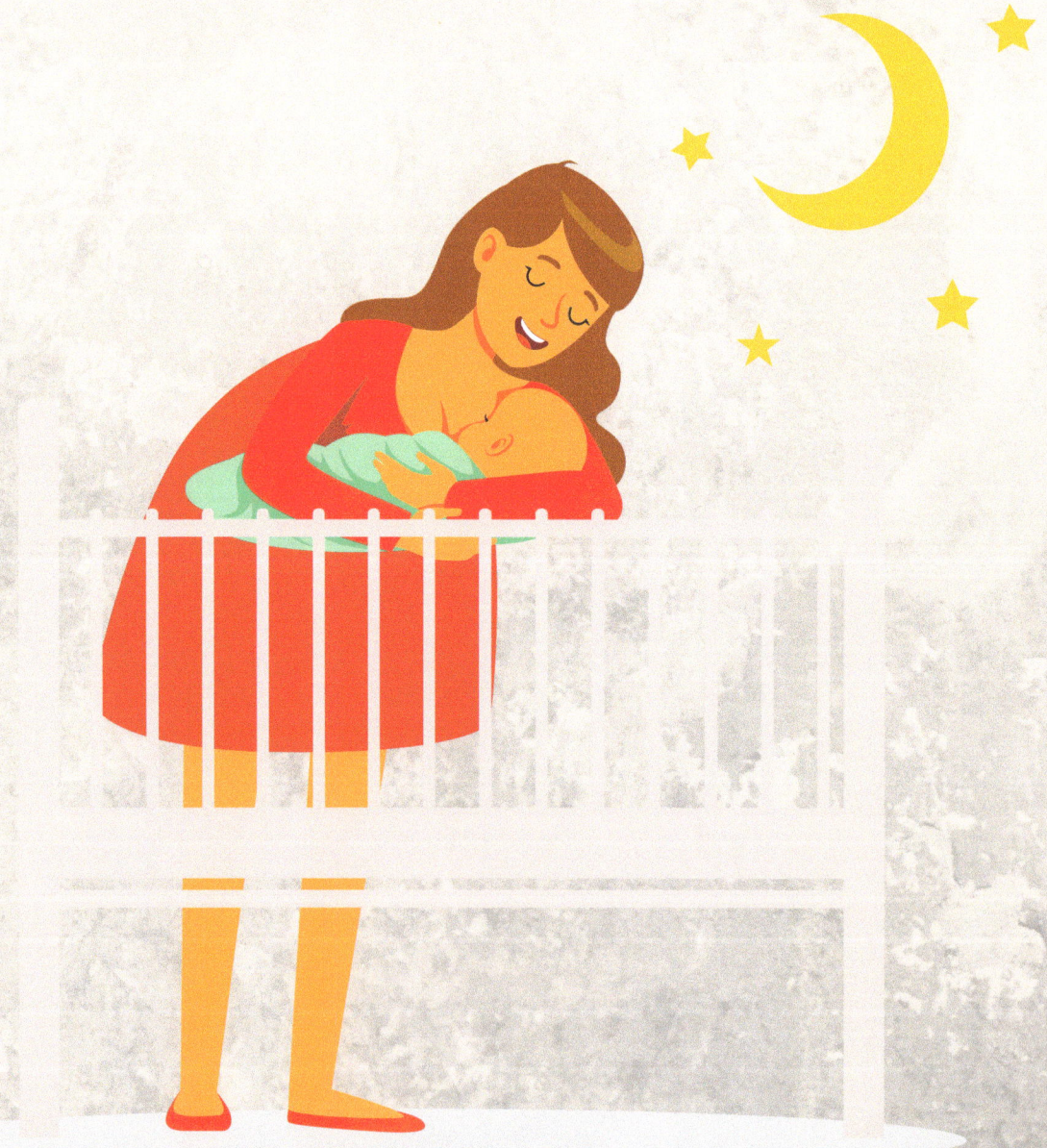

With each verse she read aloud, a sense of calm settled over the tiny nursery, and soon, Emily's cries were replaced by soft coos of delight.

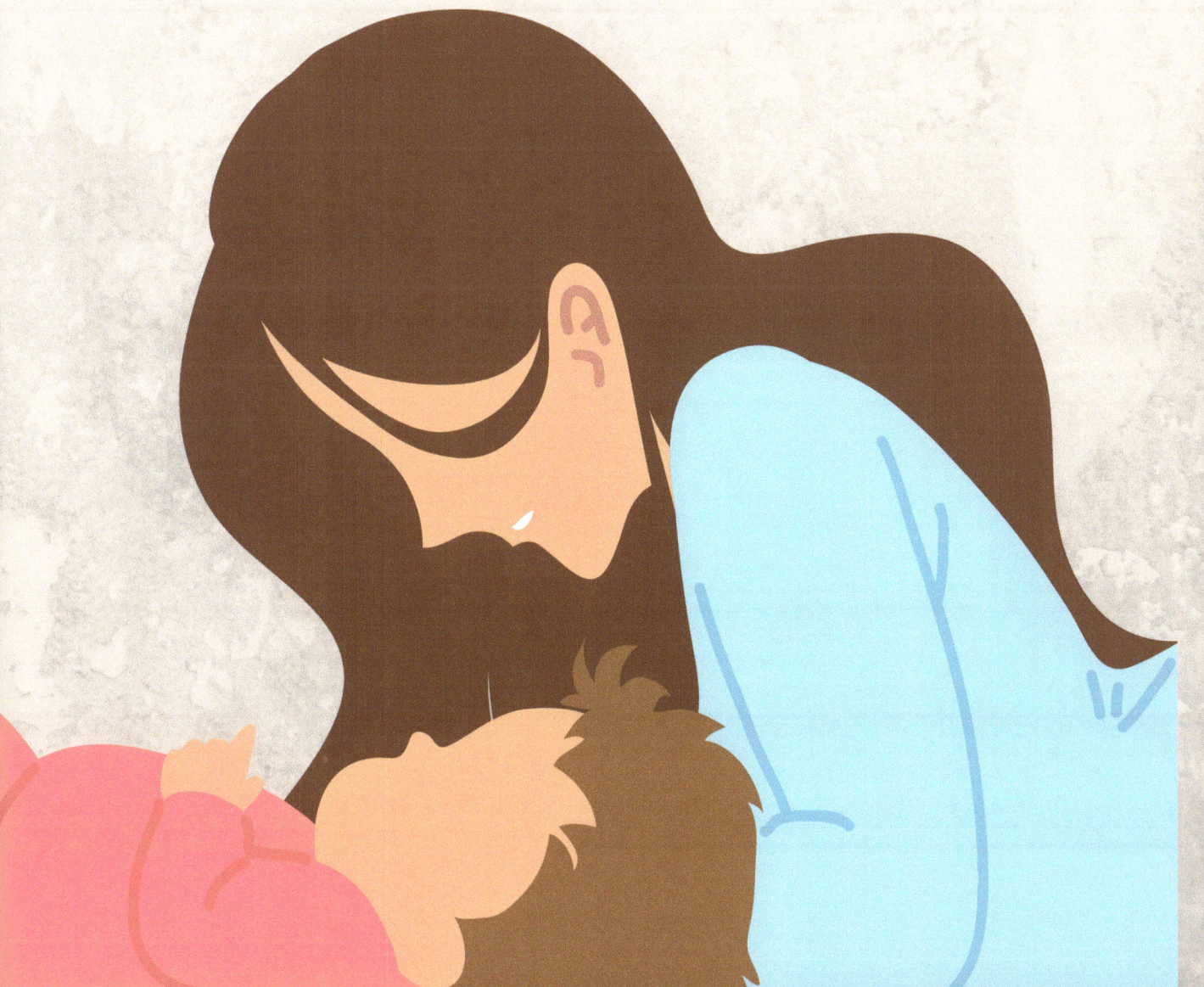

From that night onward, the Book of Baby Magic became a cherished part of Lily and Emily's bedtime routine.

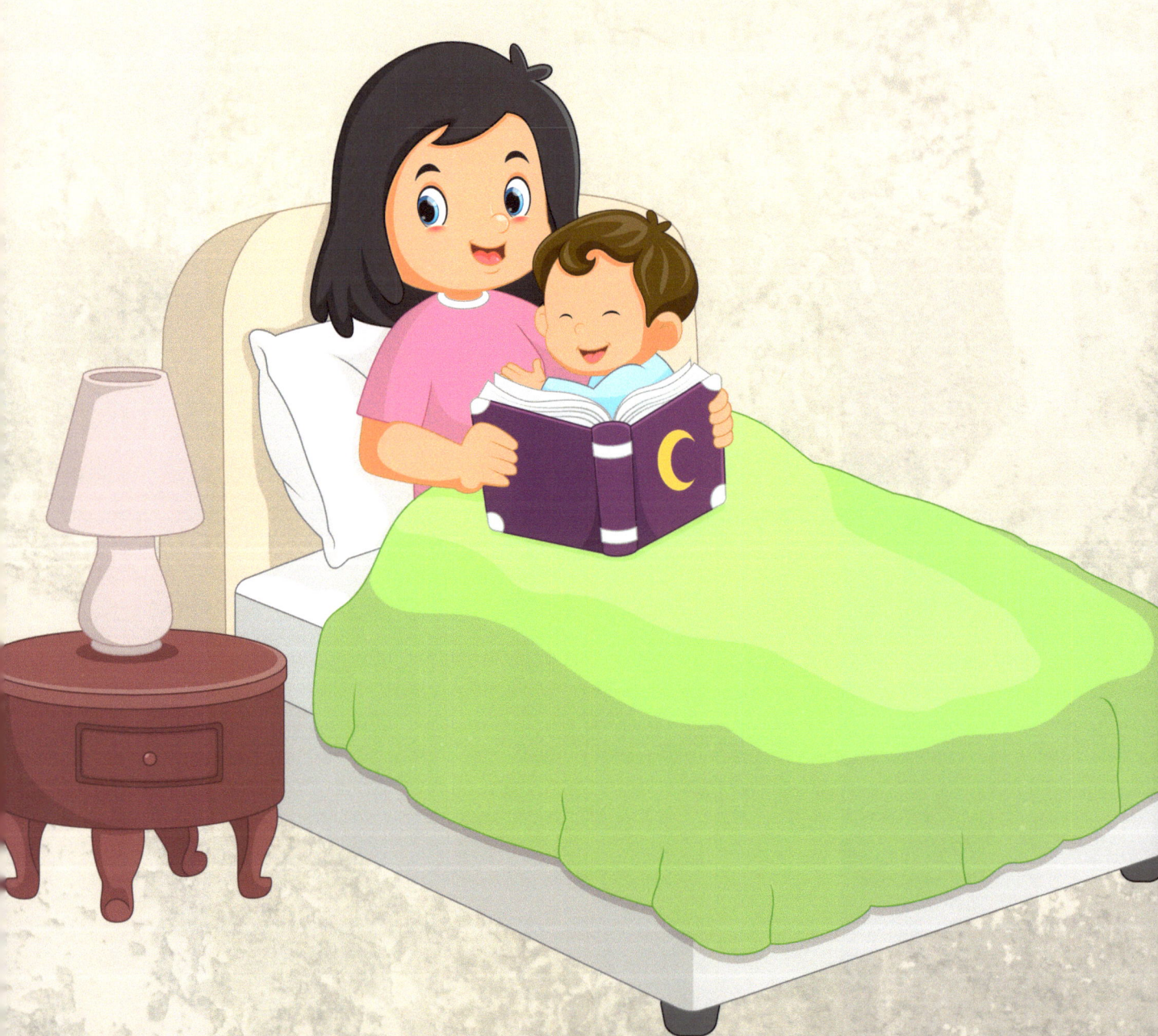

Together, they would delve into its pages, exploring the wonders of a world filled with moonlit dreams and starlit skies.

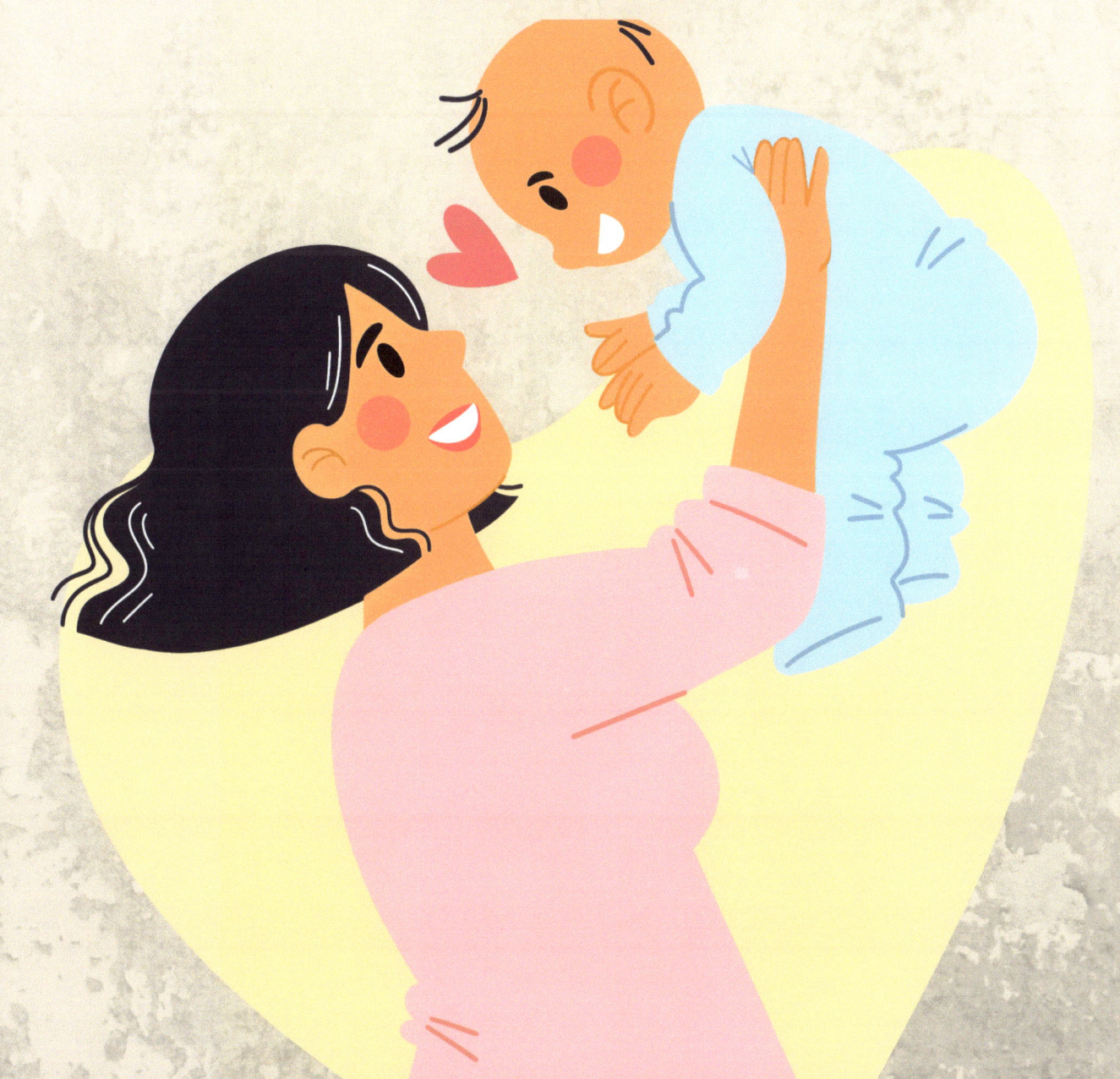

And as the years passed, the whispers of Elderwood Mysteries grew fainter, but the magic of the book endured, passed down from generation to generation, weaving its gentle spells into the hearts of babes and parents alike, for all eternity.

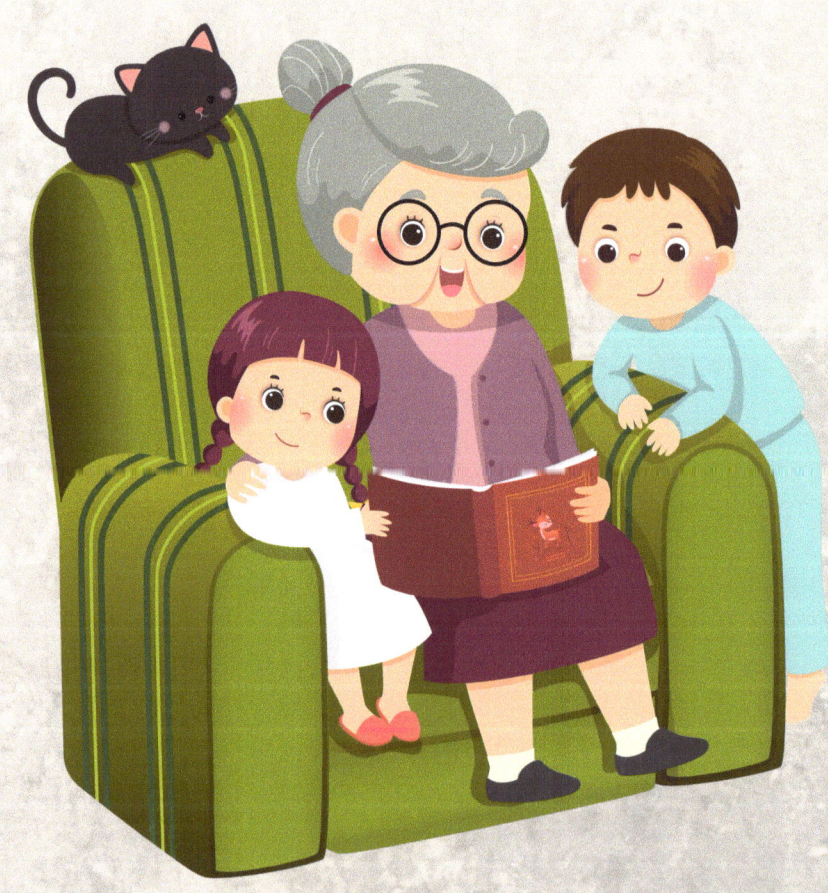

Conclusion:-

Telling bedtime stories to a child at his early age is a healthy habit and nighttime activity for their early mental development.
For the rest of their lives, it will assist them in learning moral principles.

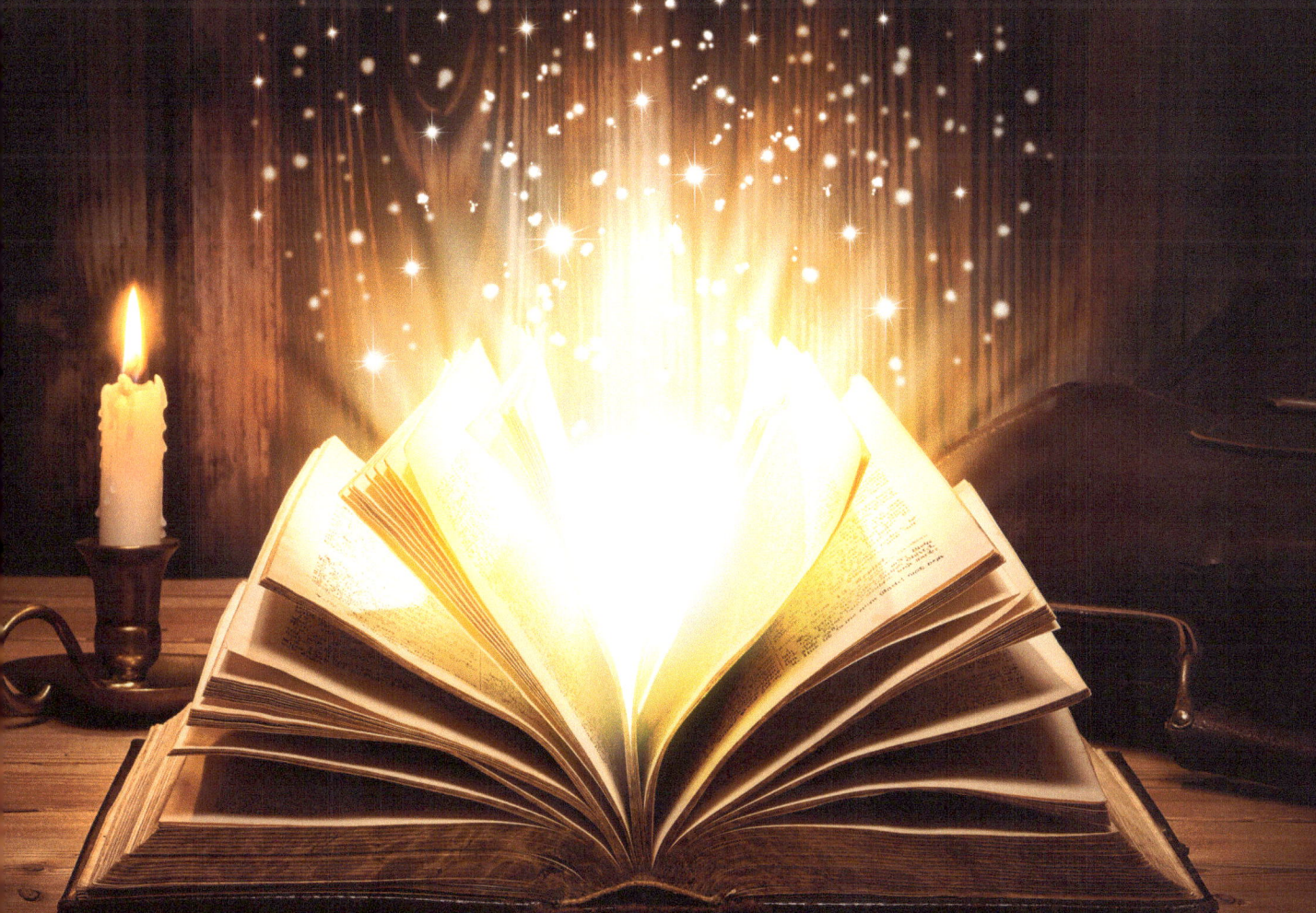

Chapter 2
Oliver's mysterious finding

Illustration:-
The beginning of the chapter describes how, after reading the enigmatic book, a youngster who had previously lived in his own fantasy world began to see the actual world.

This tale is a realistic example of how magic still exists everywhere; all you need to do is figure out how to harness it.

The true existence of magic is in your heart, just listen to your heart and follow the steps. It will help you overcome all the adventures of life.

A tiny child named Oliver used to dwell in a charming little village tucked away between hushing woodlands and undulating hills.

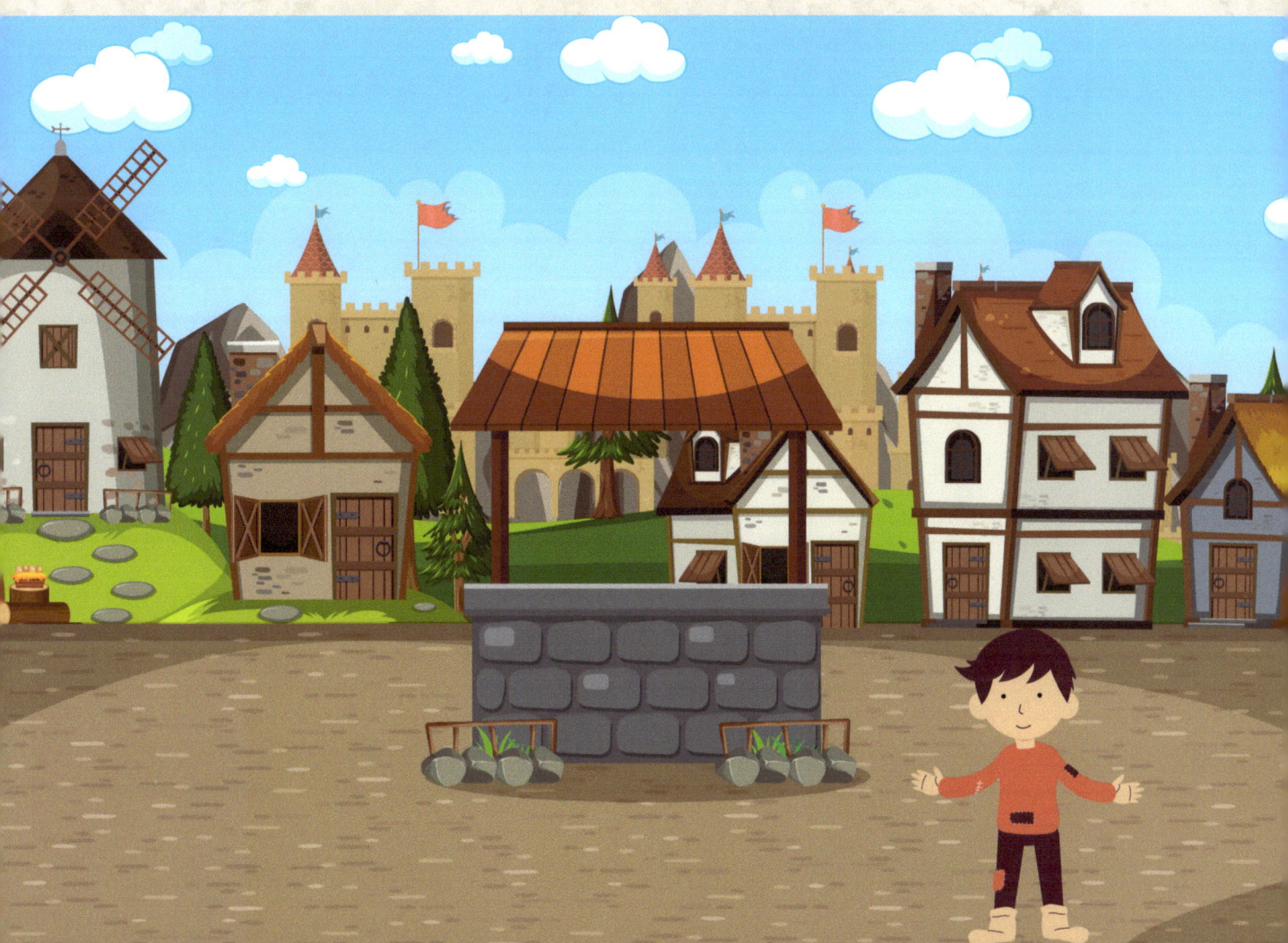

Oliver was an inquisitive boy with a mind full of fantasy and a heart full of wonder. He dreamed of amazing adventures and spent his days roaming the woods and climbing trees.

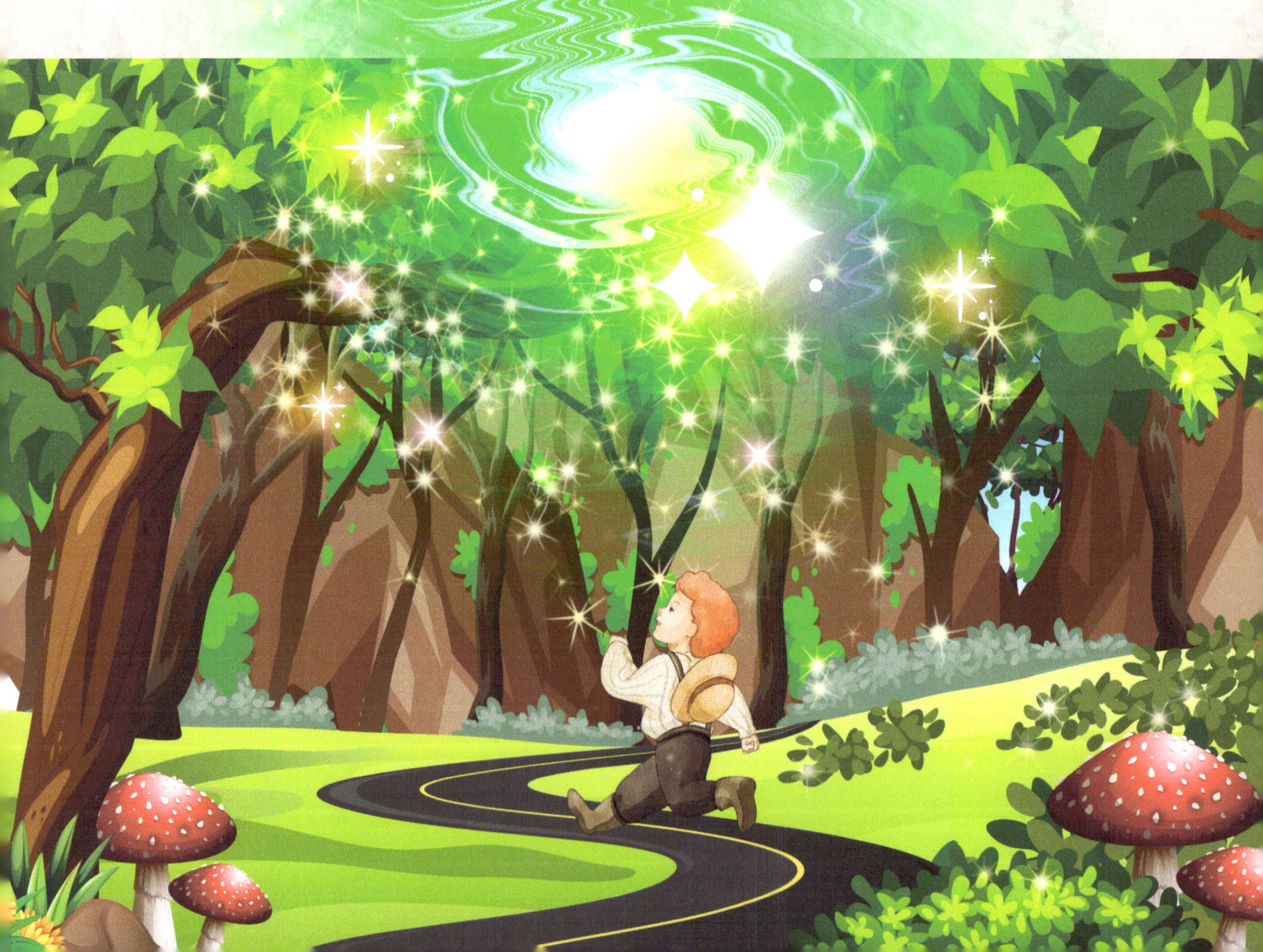

Oliver came found an old-looking book half-buried beneath a tangle of ivy one bright afternoon while meandering through the forest.

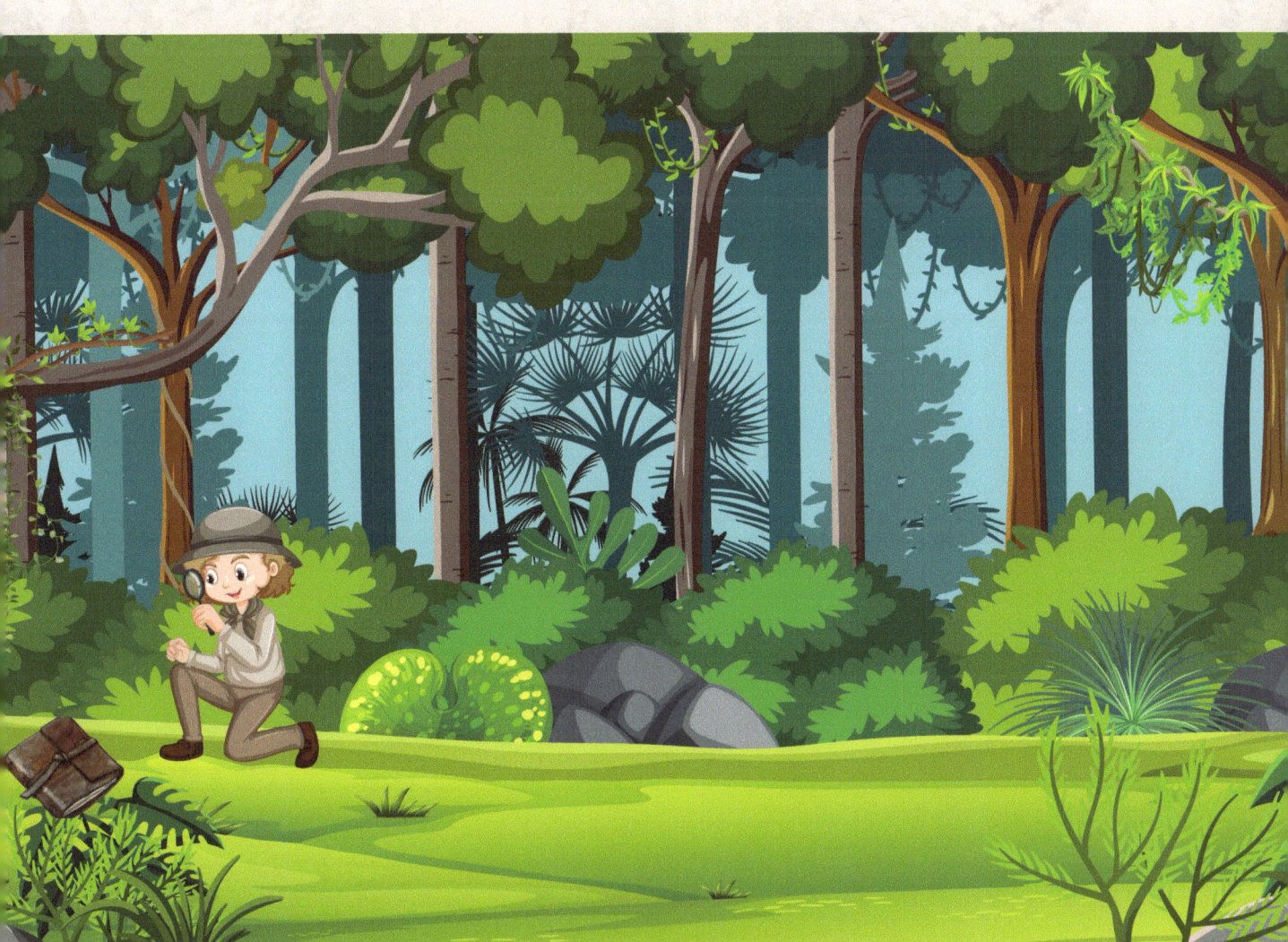

He wiped away the dirt, intrigued, and gently opened its tattered pages. The book was a magnificent storybook full of fantastical tales, much to his surprise. It wasn't just any old book!

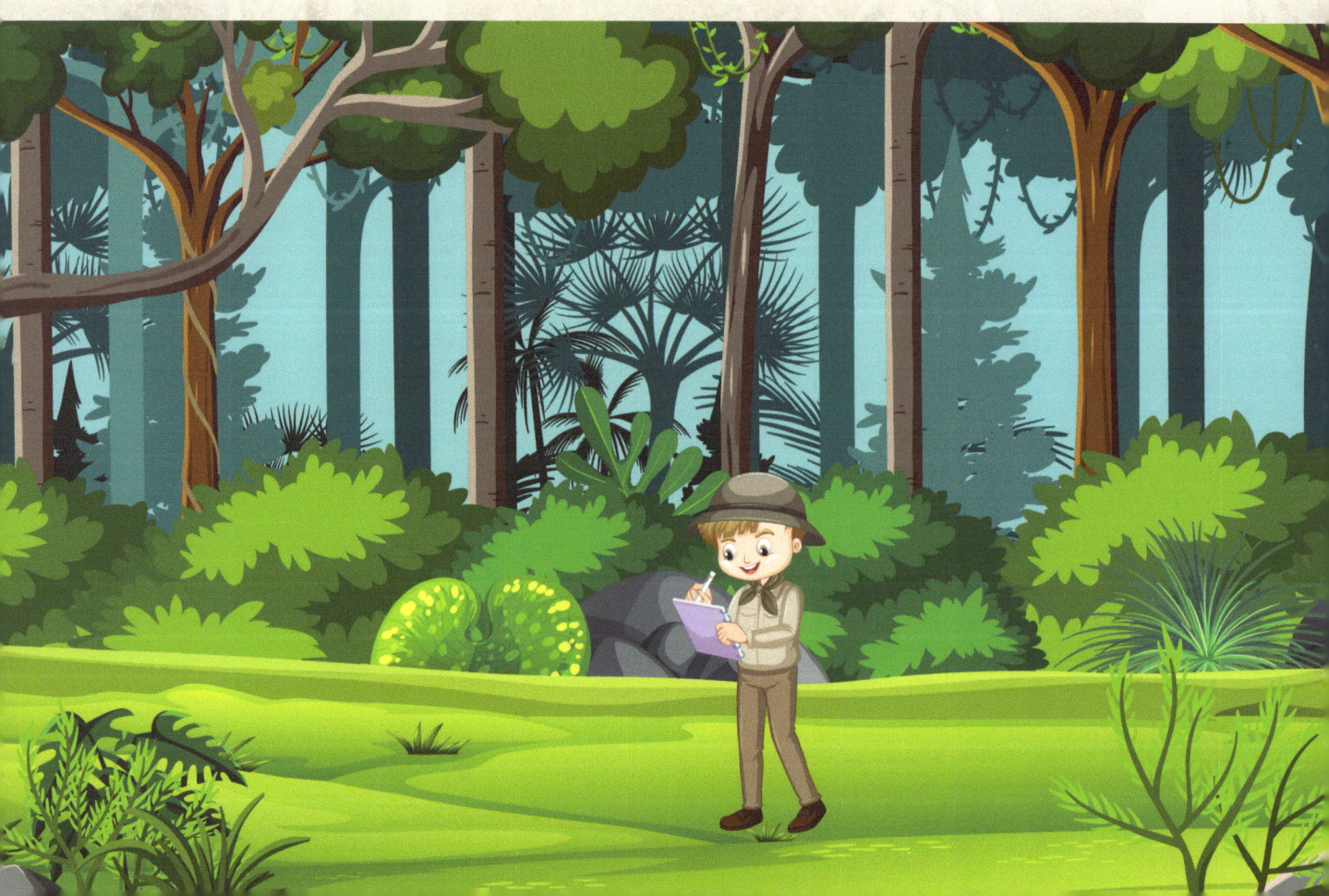

Oliver raced home and slipped himself into bed, excited to explore the beautiful world within the book, full of excitement over his unexpected treasure.

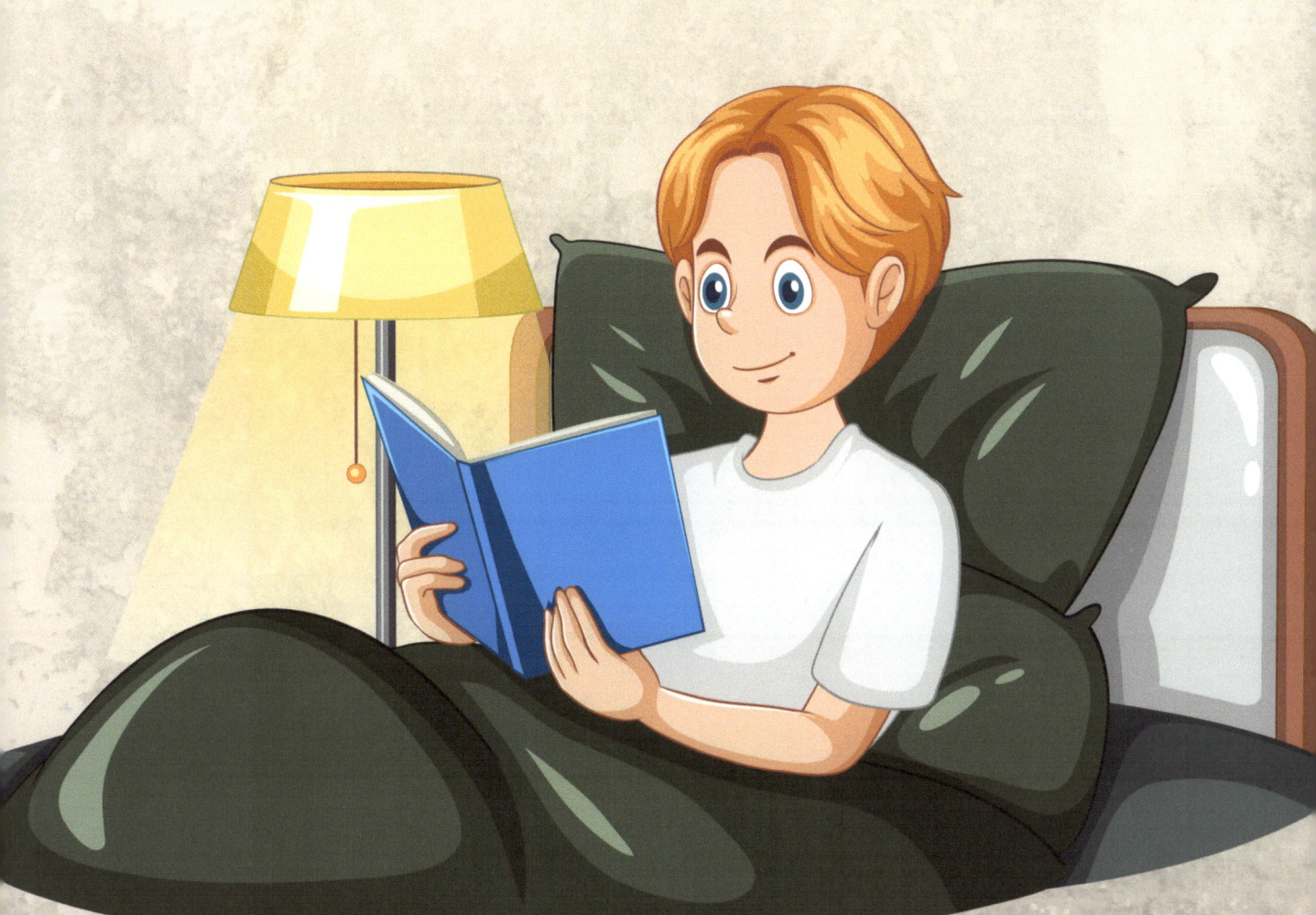

Oliver set out on numerous adventures of his own with the assistance of his newfound friends—a courageous knight, a perceptive wizard, and a cunning fairy.

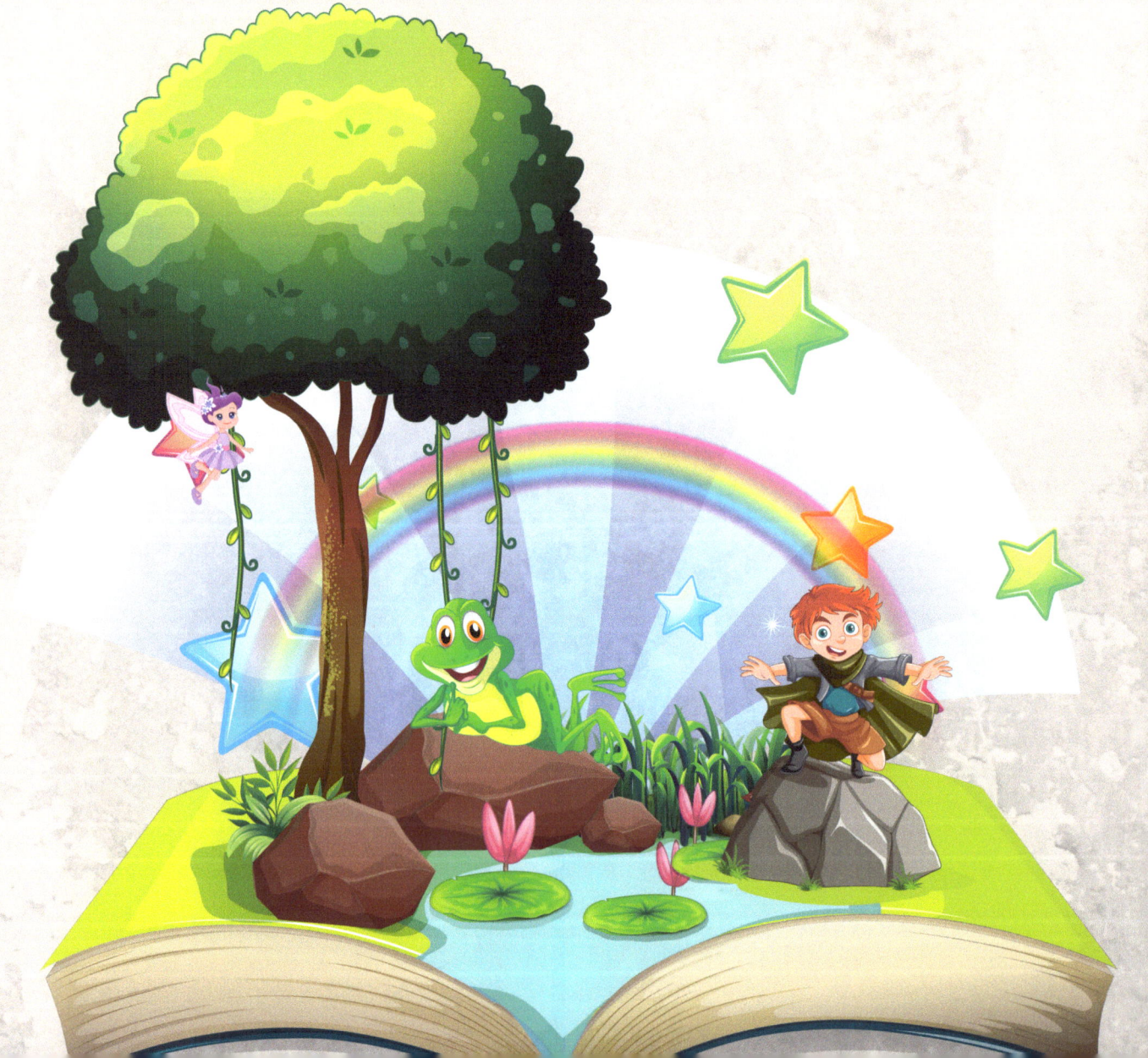

In one tale, he set out with a band of daring adventurers to locate a secret treasure that was concealed from view and protected by traps and puzzles.

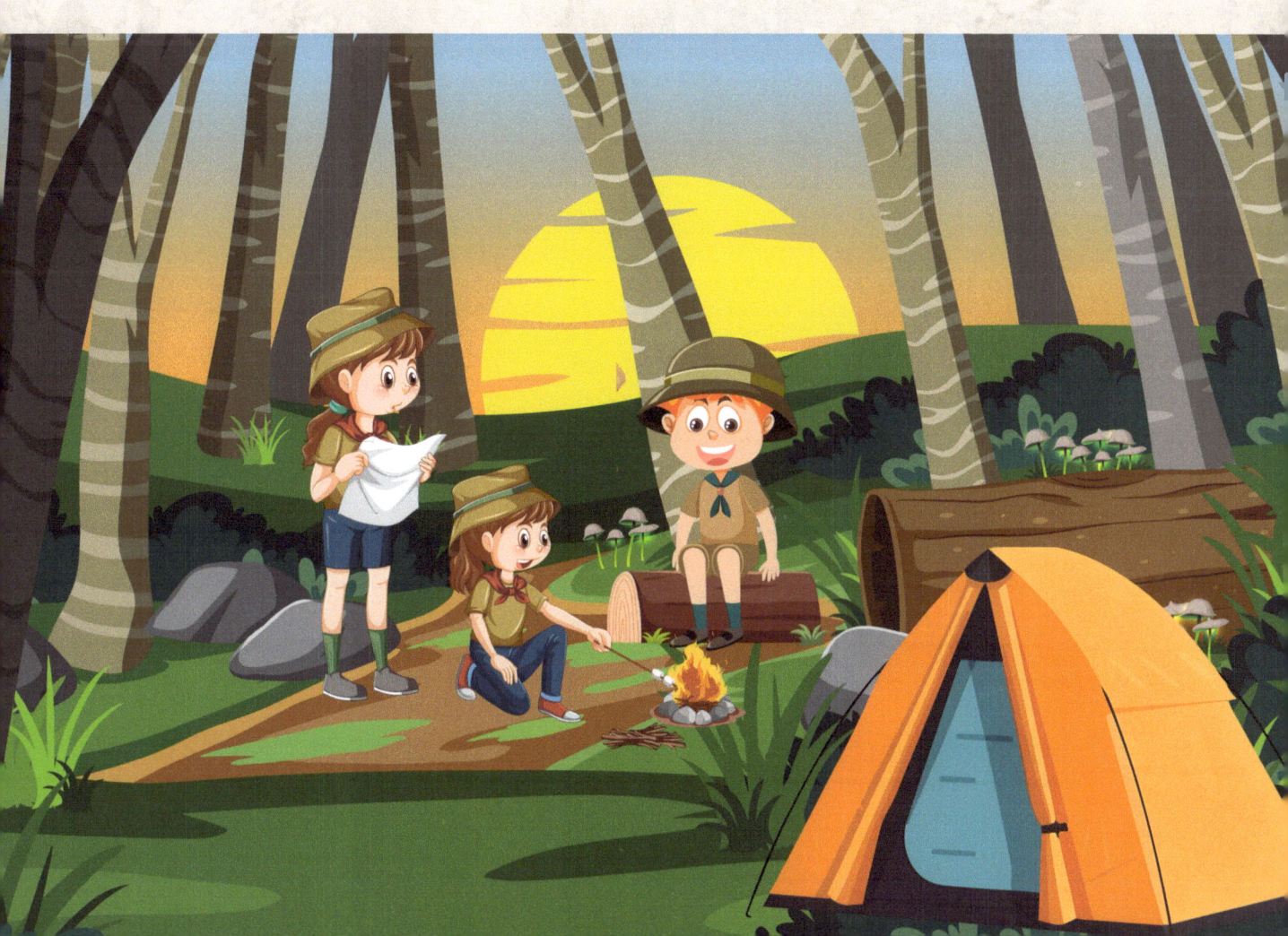

In another, he galloped across sparkling flower meadows atop the back of a magnificent unicorn.

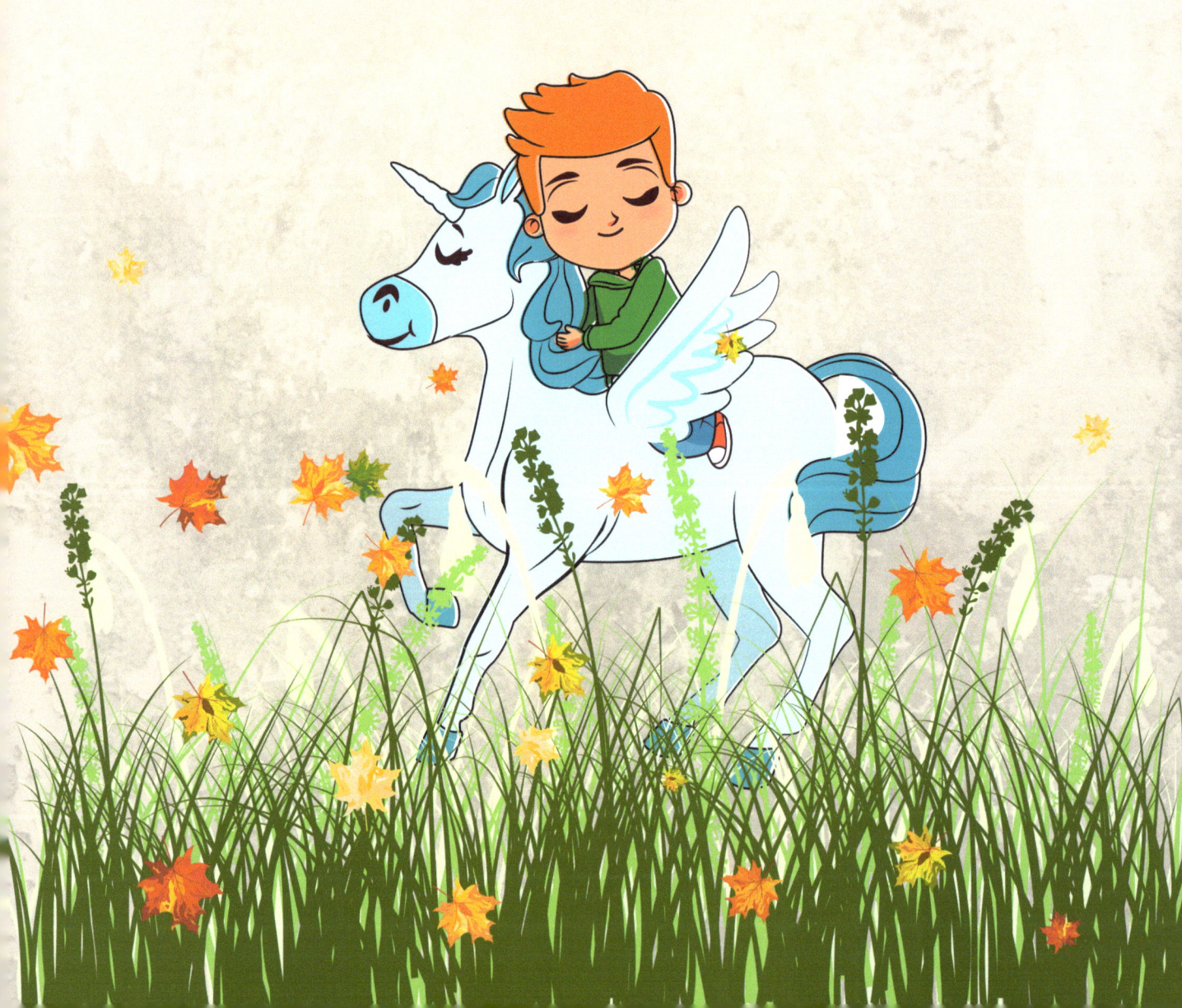

He was taken to faraway places where everything was conceivable with every page turn.

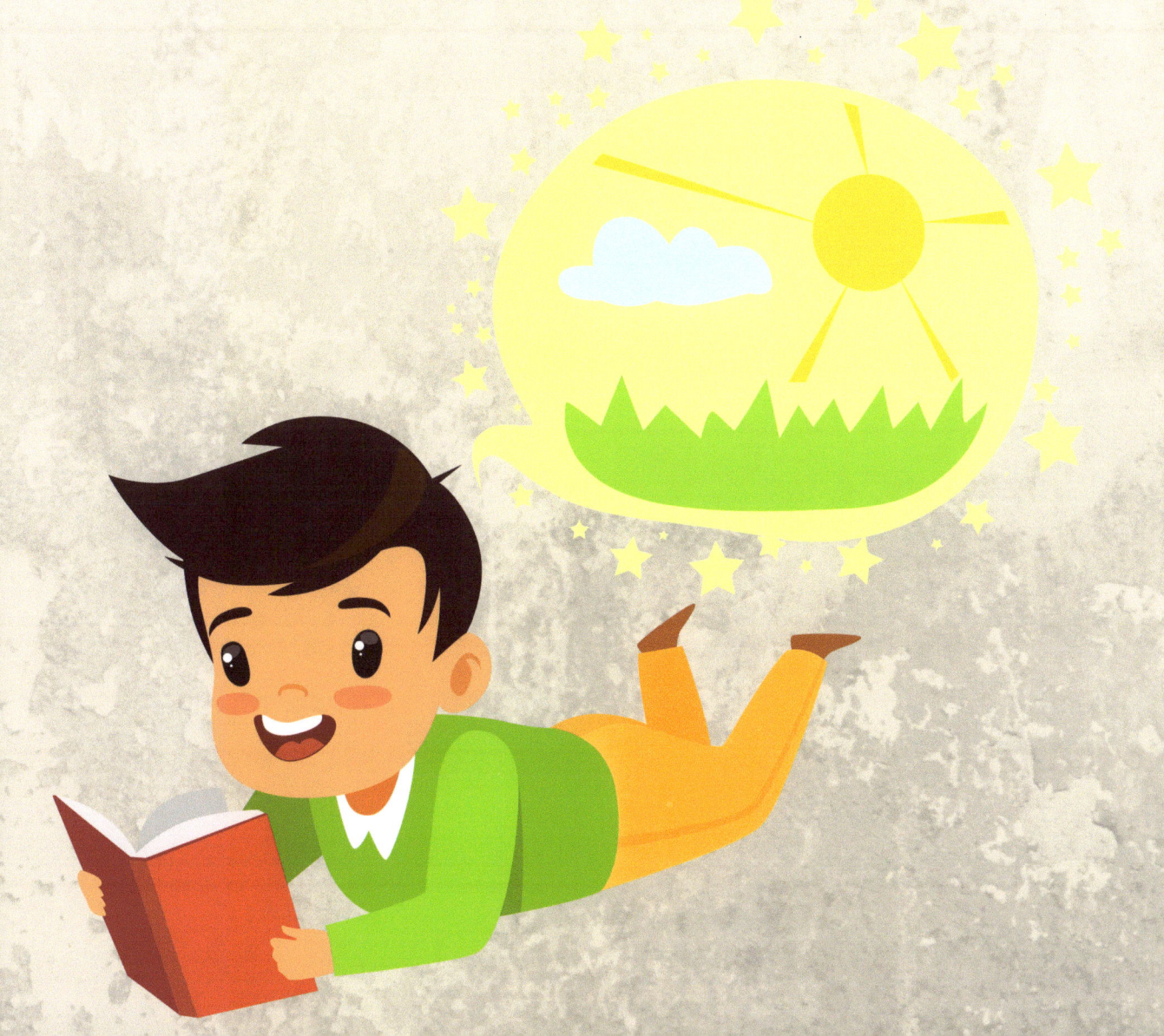

Oliver turned the pages and read tales of fearless knights fighting fearsome dragons, cunning fairies fulfilling wishes, and fearless explorers venturing into unknown territories.

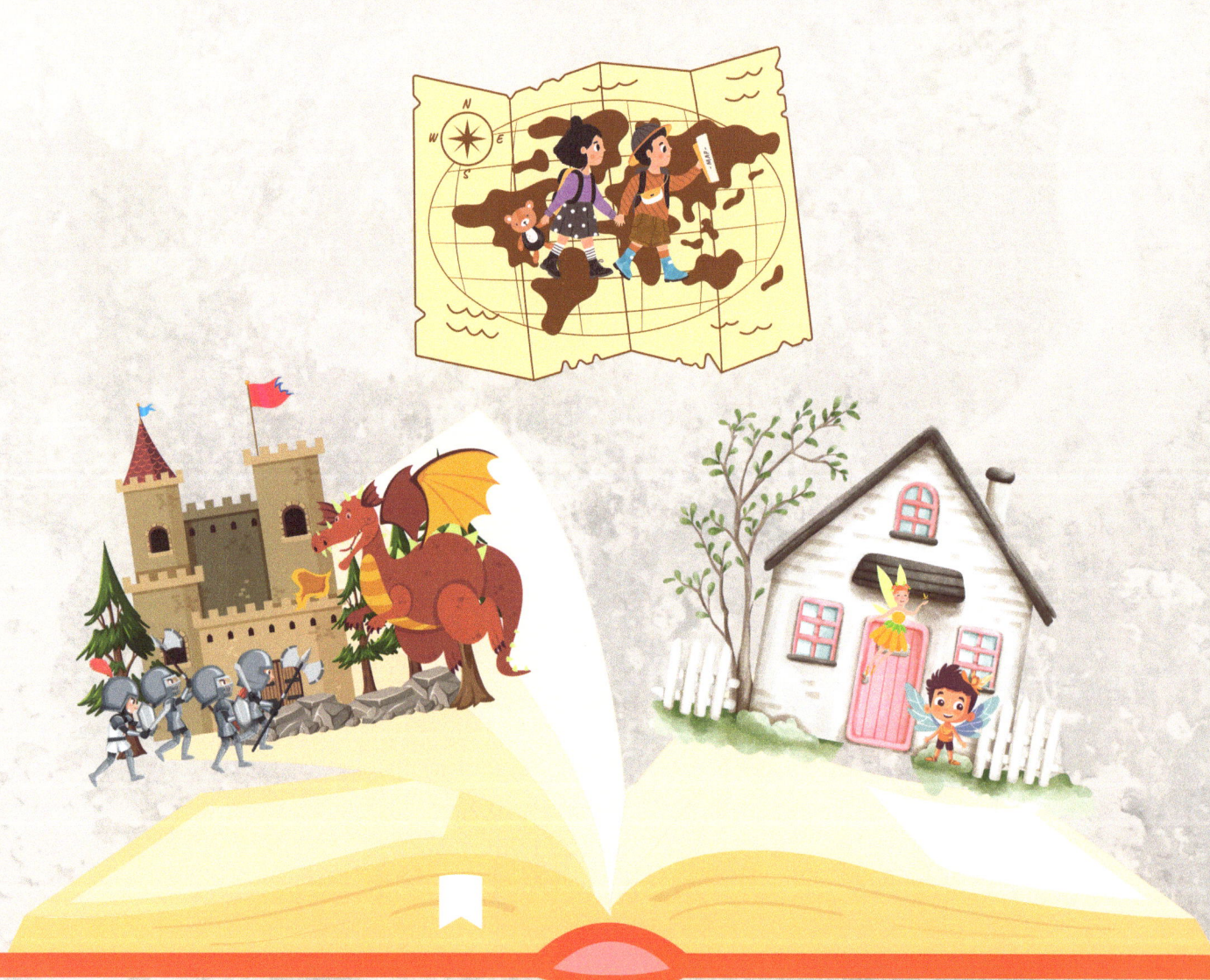

With lively graphics and engrossing words that danced before his eyes, every page appeared to come to life.

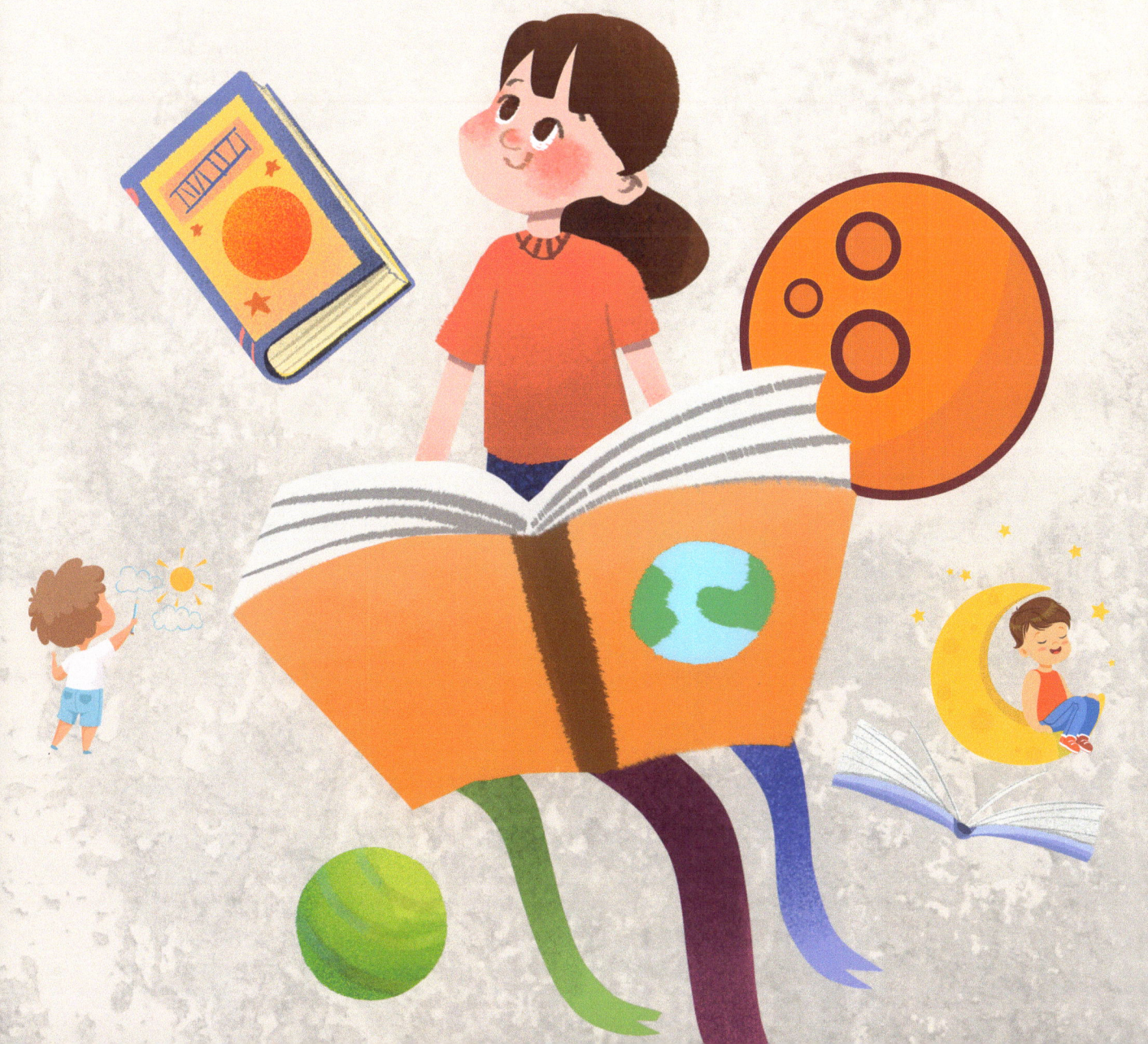

They overcame terrifying creatures, deciphered archaic mysteries, and realized the genuine value of bravery and camaraderie.

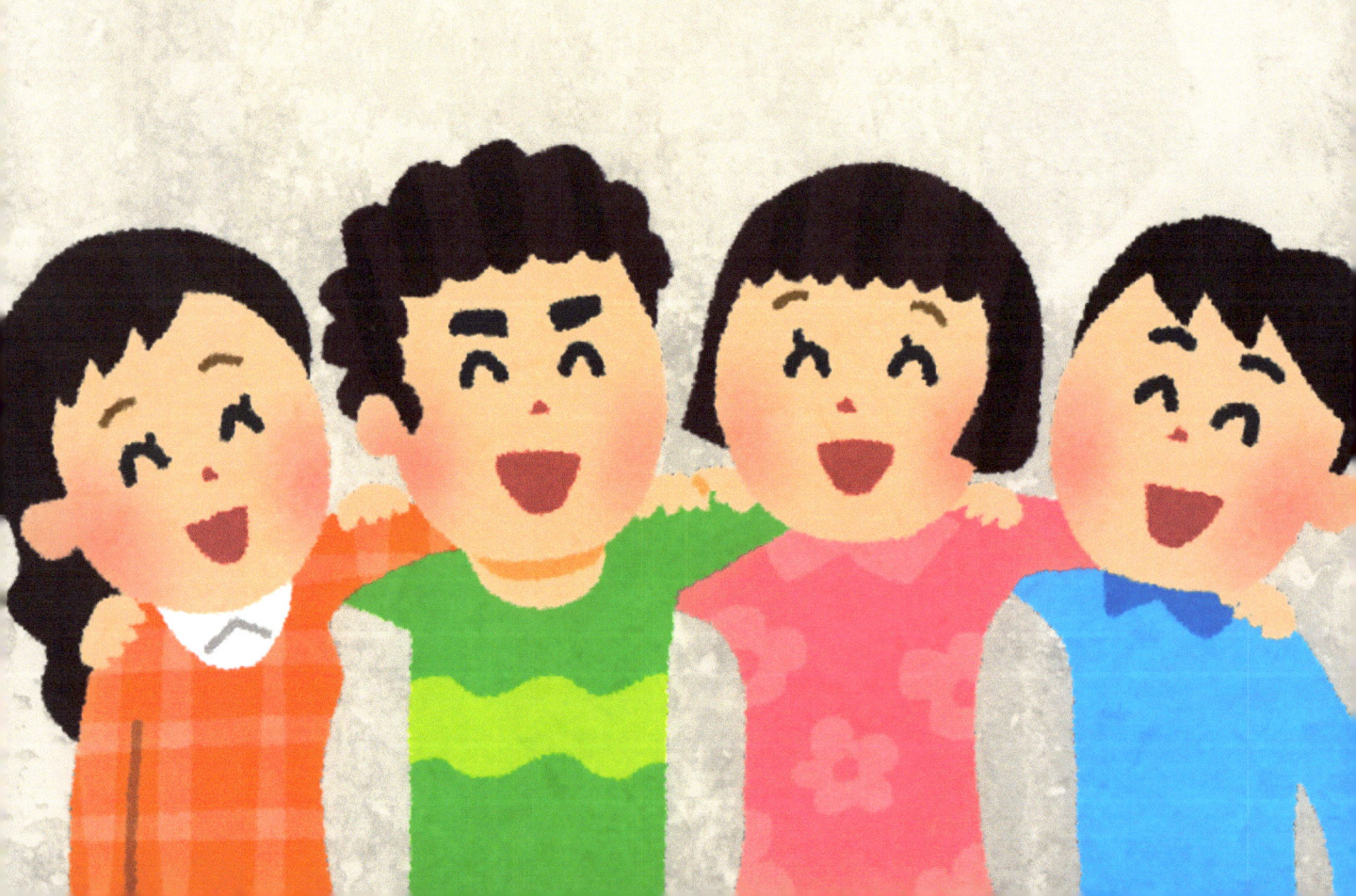

However, as Oliver read through the book more, he came to understand that the stories' true power lay in the way they ignited his own creativity.

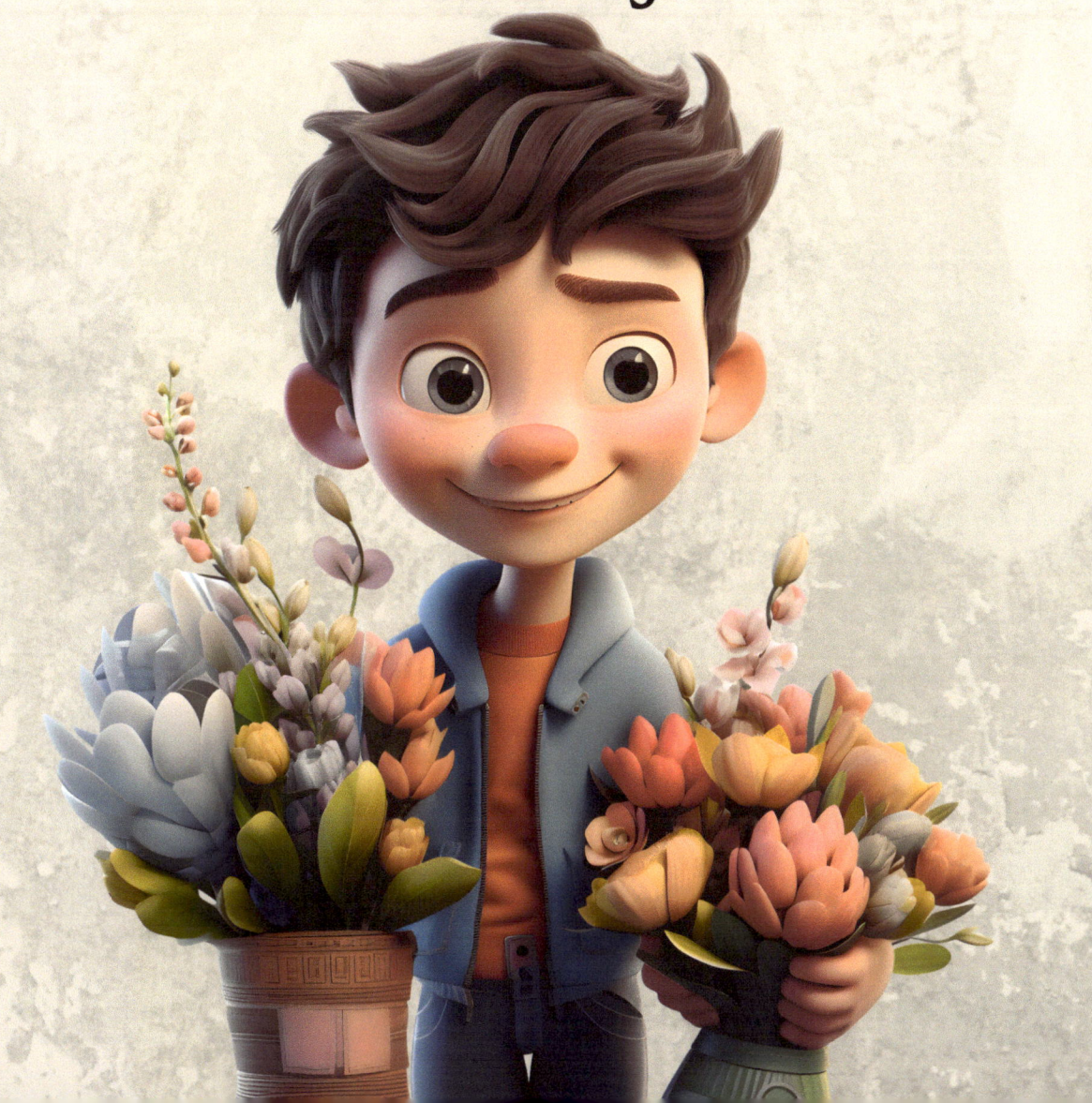

Because in an infinitely creative world, the most exciting journeys were the ones we dared to dream up.

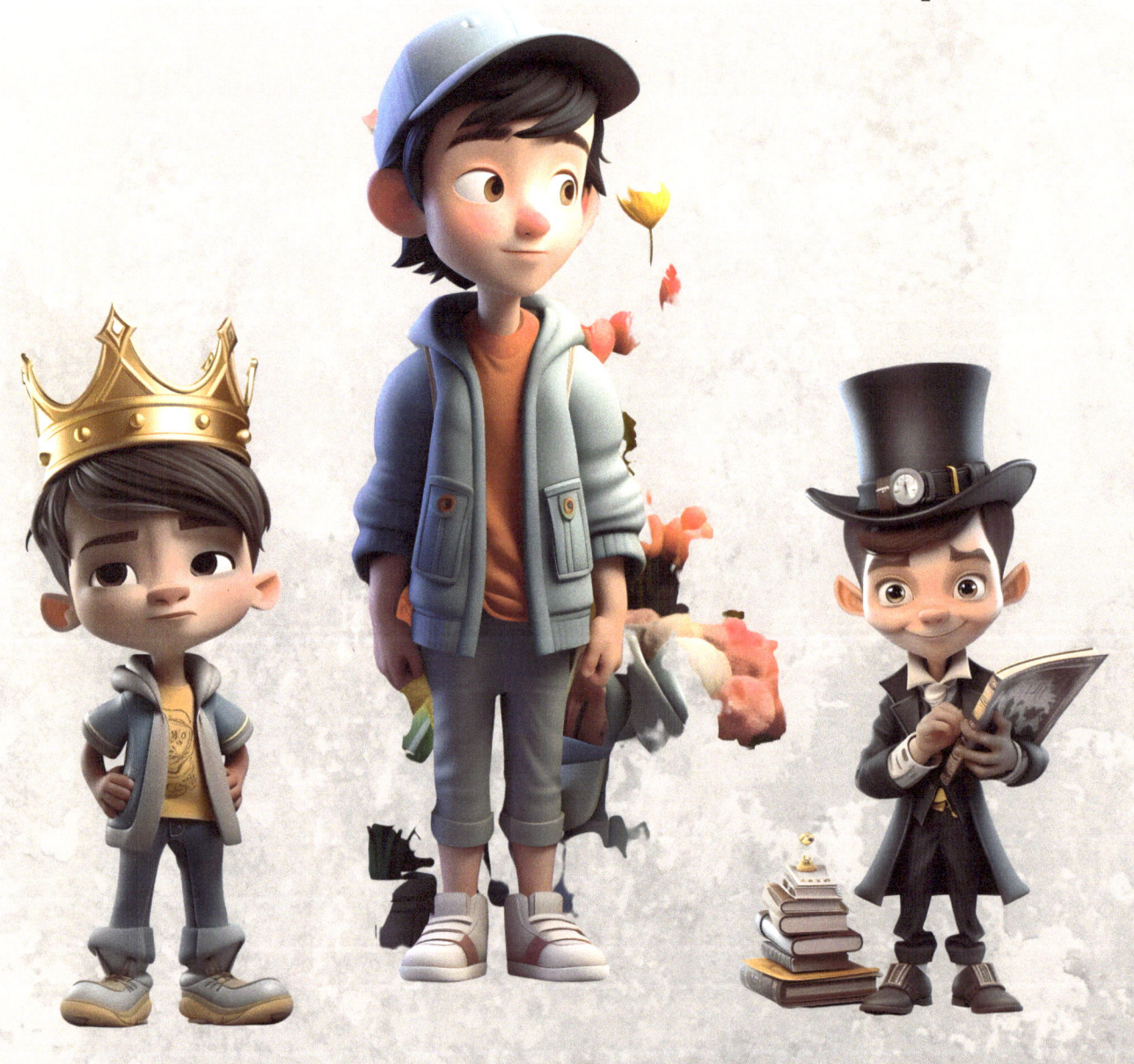

Oliver started to dream of his own adventures after being moved by the bravery of the heroes and the splendor of the enchanted countries.

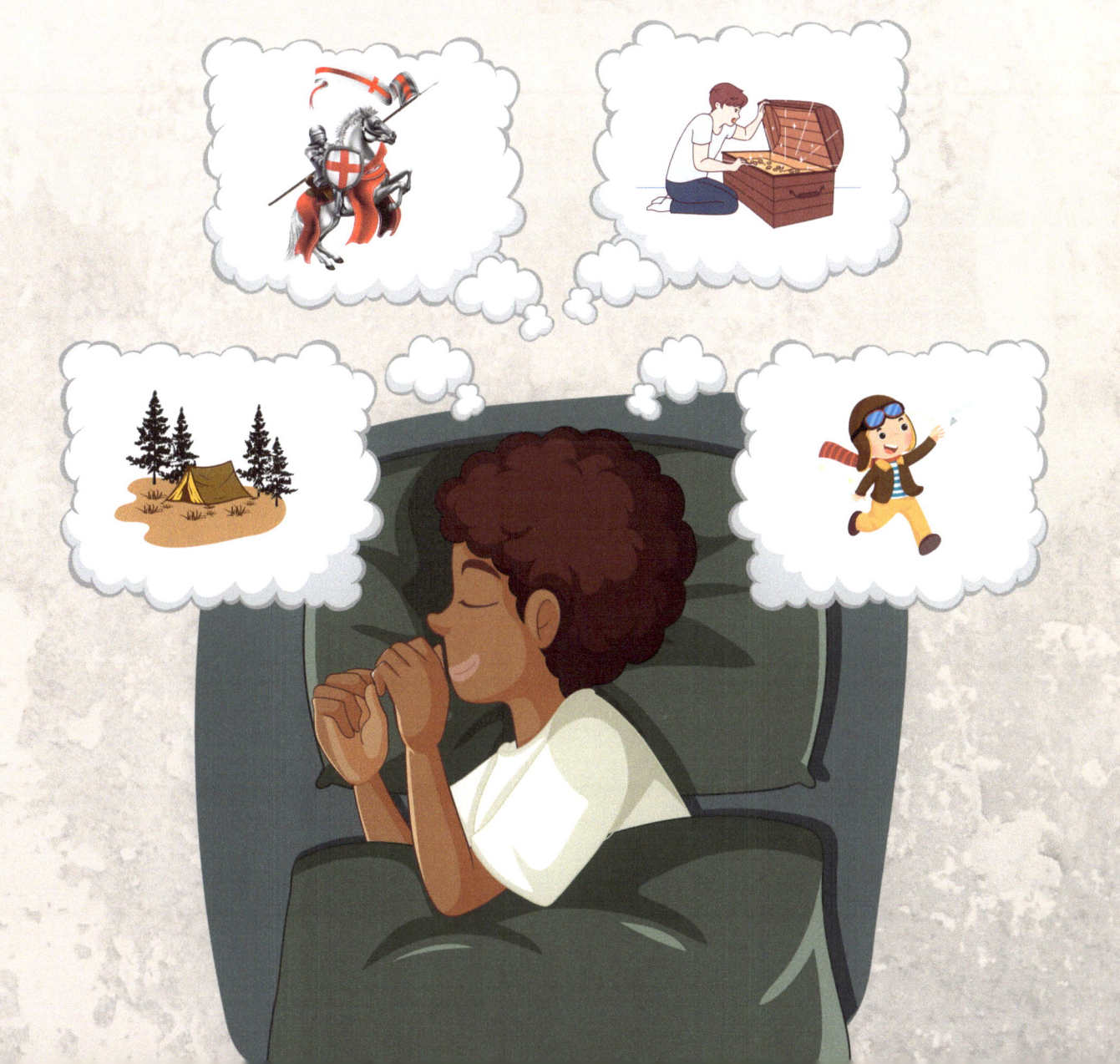

Oliver realized that even though the magical storybook's pages will eventually come to an end, the magic would never truly fade from his heart.

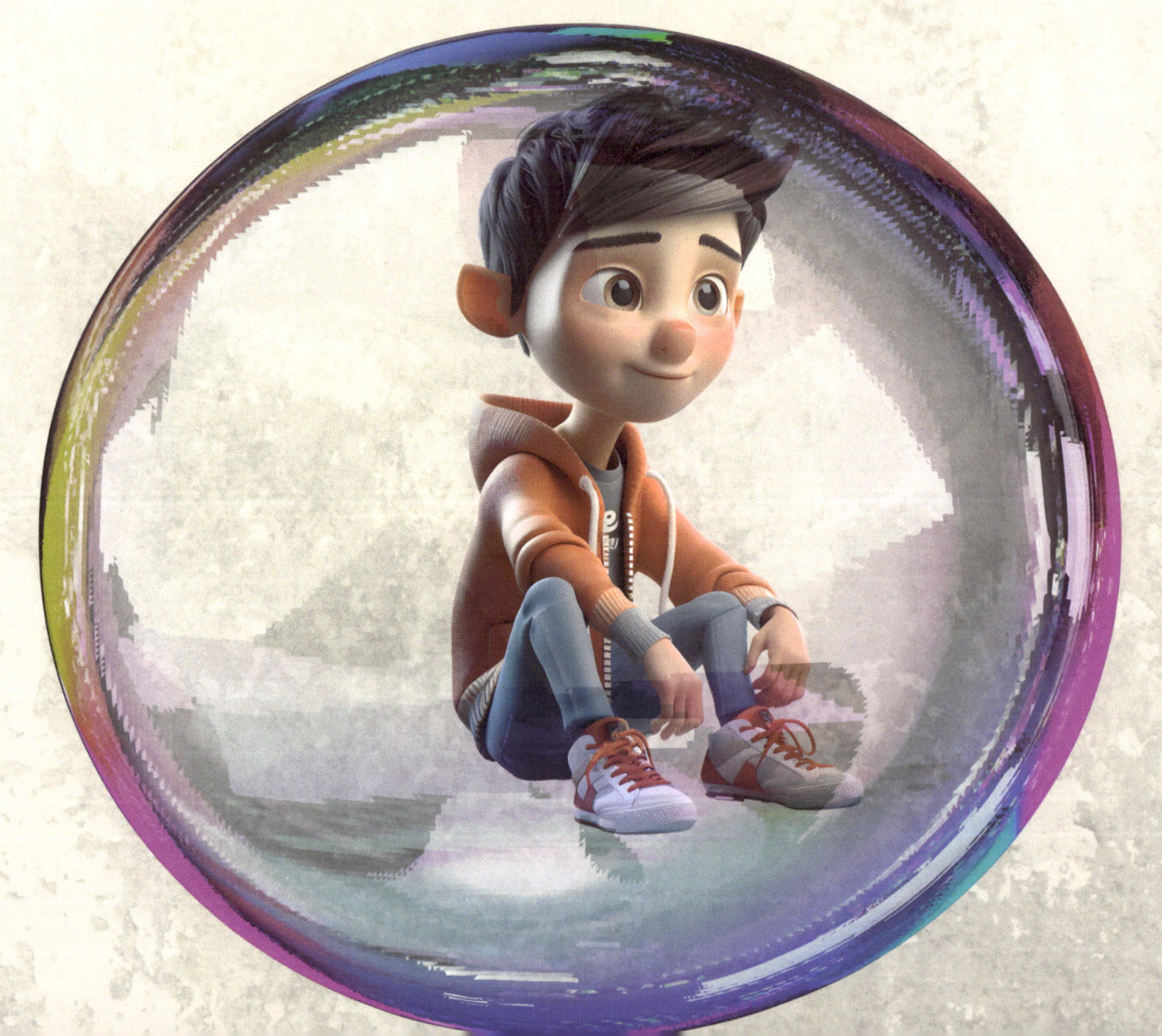

Conclusion:-

You must work through life's mysteries on your own. No made-up world can make your fantasies come true even if you accomplish nothing at all. Though dreams do exist, you should have the bravery and ability to realize them.

While having dreams is perfectly acceptable, it is important to follow through on your dreams.

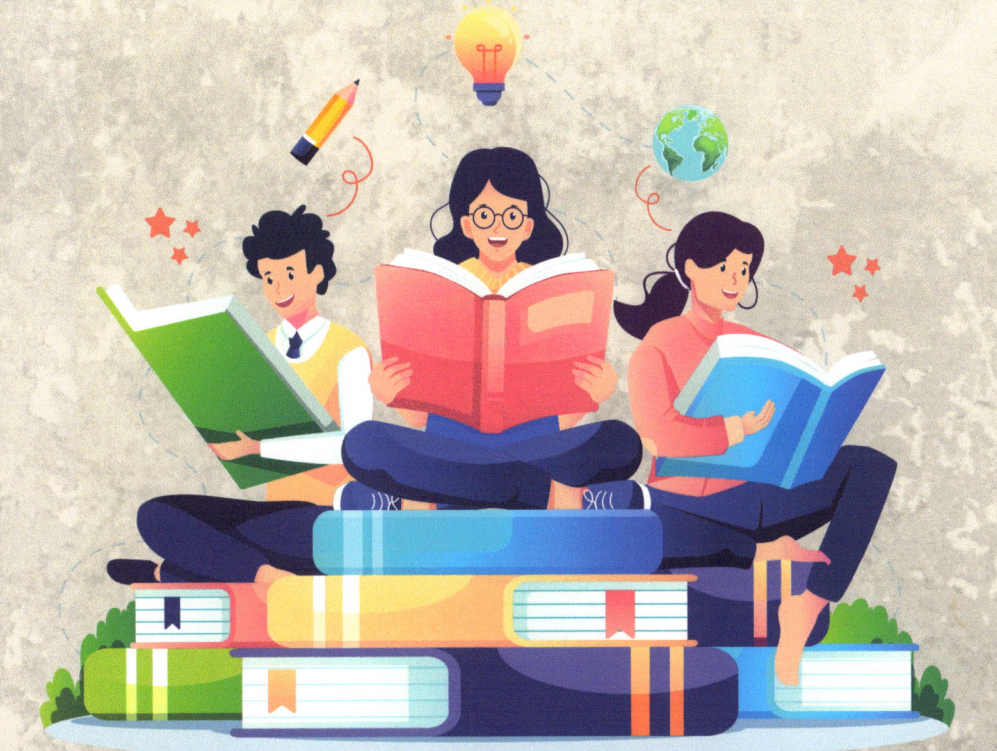

www.ingramcontent.com/pod-product-compliance
Lightning Source LLC
Chambersburg PA
CBHW042028230526
45474CB00006B/43